# 30 Days
## to a More Incredible
### *You*

from *Today's Christian Woman* magazine

Compiled and Edited by
RAMONA CRAMER TUCKER

Tyndale House Publishers, Inc.
WHEATON, ILLINOIS

**Library of Congress Cataloging-in-Publication Data**

30 days to a more incredible you / edited by Ramona Cramer Tucker.
    p.    cm.
  "TCW books from Today's Christian woman magazine."
  ISBN 0-8423-0592-0 (sc)
  1. Christian women—Prayer-books and devotions—English. 2. Christian women—Religious life. I. Tucker, Ramona Cramer.
BV4844.A125 1998
242'.643—dc21                98-23841

Printed in the United States of America

03  02  01
10  9  8  7  6  5

# CONTENTS

# INTRODUCTION

$\mathcal{D}$o you ever wish

- you could better control your schedule?
- you knew what to do when loneliness creeps up on you?
- you could forgive—and then move on?
- you could make friends more easily?
- you didn't fall into the trap of negativism so quickly?

If we're honest, we all wish we could improve ourselves in certain areas. We wonder why God didn't create us with a size-eight figure or the ability to speak before crowds without our knees knocking. We wish we could be all things to all people—until we realize that we're just one person with finite time and energy.

This book provides perspective for a range of your "self" questions, including, "How can I cultivate contentment in my life?" "How can I best handle life on the whirl?" "How do I overcome the comparison trap?" And, maybe most important, "How can I find time for a *real* break—just for me?"

Each day provides a Scripture passage; a story; a quote from a well-known person such as Jill Briscoe, Babbie Mason, Kay Arthur, or Bodie Thoene; and reflections on a topic, as well as action steps to help you improve a particular aspect of your "self life." In addition, the "Faith Focus" will help you evaluate how you're currently doing, where you'd like to be, and how you'll get there. The "Prayer Pointer" will assist you in focusing your prayers on the topic for the day.

In just thirty short days, this book will give you handholds that can transform the way you feel about yourself—and how you relate to others. And as you grow to like who you are as God's specially gifted child even more, you'll become convinced that the Lord's message to Jeremiah is also an encouragement and challenge to *you*: "I knew you before I formed you in your mother's womb. Before you were born I set you apart and appointed you as my spokesman to the world" (Jer. 1:5)!

Ramona Cramer Tucker
Editor
*Today's Christian Woman* magazine

I KNOW HOW TO LIVE ON ALMOST NOTHING OR WITH EVERYTHING. I HAVE LEARNED THE SECRET OF LIVING IN EVERY SITUATION, WHETHER IT IS WITH A FULL STOMACH OR EMPTY, WITH PLENTY OR LITTLE. FOR I CAN DO EVERYTHING WITH THE HELP OF CHRIST WHO GIVES ME THE STRENGTH I NEED.

PHILIPPIANS 4:12-13

DAY 1

- *I wish I had her job.*
- *It would be nice to have new carpet.*
- *If I had more money, I'd dress like that too.*

If you've thought any of the above, you're not alone—especially in a culture that judges who we are by what we have. But there's one Person who doesn't judge us that way—our Lord Jesus Christ. And in Philippians 4:12-13 the apostle Paul says he is content with what he has (and what he doesn't have). Here's how to get over "never enough" and be satisfied with "what is."

# Cultivating Contentment

There's a lot in my life I wish I could change. I'm not miserable—but I struggle with being satisfied. One Scripture that makes me squirm is the apostle Paul's reminder to Timothy: "So if we have enough food and clothing, let us be content" (1 Tim. 6:8). I have food, but too often it's macaroni and cheese. I have clothing, but looking through the L. L. Bean catalog brings out materialistic urges. I have furniture, but it resembles estate-sale treasures more than Crate-and-Barrel chic. Often I'd like more—and better. And that's just the beginning of my discontent.

I've met other women who struggle with the same conflict. My neighbor Jackie, the mother of teens, tells me her level of contentment fluctuates. "It depends on our finances, the state of the house, my husband's and kids' moods, and whether or not I have PMS," she says. Another friend, a single parent, would love to pull up stakes and move to Florida after her youngest is through school. She's tired of her job, tired of winter, eager to make a fresh start by the sea.

It's so easy to get caught in the "never enough" spiral—always wanting a bigger house, more money, a different or more prestigious job. The problem is, many of us define contentment as that ideal state of constant happiness where every problem is solved and every goal is met. But what happens when you achieve a goal? It's like yanking dandelions—you pull one, and another pops up in its place.

Ten years ago, I had a certain sum in mind as my ideal annual income. I thought, *If only I could earn that, my financial woes would be over.* But when I reached that magic number, it no longer seemed ideal, thanks to inflation. What I thought would make me content didn't satisfy me any longer.

I've learned that we'll never solve all our problems this side of eternity. New dreams will always replace the old—and that can be good. My friend Judy observes, "If you feel you've achieved everything, you'll never grow. You'll have no motivation, no edge."

*If you wear thankfulness, you'll be too busy counting your blessings to complain. Plus, it's very attractive. People love to be with a positive person.*
MARY WHELCHEL

Ultimately, there's no true contentment apart from knowing, loving, and desiring to follow Christ. As the apostle Paul says: "I have learned the secret of living in every situation" (Phil. 4:12). If we're honest, most of us can't say we're content in "every situation." But it is a model to aspire to, becoming more like Paul . . . more like Christ.

As we seek God's peace and ask his help in setting our minds on "things above"—no matter what the world may be throwing at us—we may be able to say, echoing the apostle Paul, "I am *learning* to be content in every circumstance." Come to think of it, that would make a great inscription for a plaque—I could hang it in my kitchen and meditate on it as I start boiling the macaroni for dinner.

*Elizabeth Cody Newenhuyse*

# A STEP FURTHER

## Keys to a Satisfying Life

1. *Let the peace of Christ be your measuring stick* (Col. 3:15). Allow yourself the gift of regularly sitting in God's presence and reminding yourself through his Word what is truly important.
2. *Hang in there.* Be patient and trust God.
3. *Give thanks.* What are you thankful for—a car that continues to run? A church home? Good health? The gift of laughter? The possibilities are endless.
4. *Arm yourself against worldly seductions.* Pray for protection from temptation. Ask a friend to hold you accountable.
5. *Move beyond yourself.* Take on a new project. Become a hospice volunteer. Challenge yourself mentally or physically. Anything that stretches you will foster contentment and give you a fresh perspective on life. ECN

## Faith Focus

Are you content with your life, or do you struggle in certain areas? If so, which ones—and why? Which of the five steps to a more satisfying life could you take today?

## Prayer Pointer

Think of five things to thank God for—and then do it, lavishly! Spend time praising him for his goodness to you in big and small ways. Then ask him to help you be more content with what he's given you—and with what he hasn't.

I WAIT QUIETLY BEFORE GOD, FOR MY HOPE IS IN HIM. HE ALONE IS MY ROCK AND MY SALVATION, MY FORTRESS WHERE I WILL NOT BE SHAKEN.

PSALM 62:5-6

*A*t nineteen I made my first trip alone anywhere—and got stranded in a foreign country for two weeks due to a transport strike. Although I'd had "alone time" before, I was intensely lonely. I'd never been in a position before where it was just God and me, with no one else to rely on.

Now I look back on that scary experience with grateful thanks. For it was during that loneliness that I, as Psalm 62:5-6 says, learned to "wait quietly" and hope in God alone.

Loneliness can be a burden—or a gift. The choice is up to you.

# When the "Lonelies" Strike

When my friend Pauline was thirty, her roommate moved away. Pauline couldn't find another, no matter how hard she tried. As she moved alone into a new apartment, Pauline felt unattached, vulnerable, lonely, and afraid for her safety.

One day I shared with her my own battle with loneliness, which began with a phone call from my doctor explaining that my husband, Rick, and I would probably never conceive a child. The deep sense of loss and grief we felt was expected. What surprised me was the profound loneliness I felt for the children I would never have.

We all feel lonely at times. Even if we work hard to establish healthy habits and to serve God and neighbor, loneliness can surface again and again over the years. This isn't a matter for shame any more than cancer or a broken bone would be; it's simply a fact of a fallen world. The death of a loved one, a divorce, a romantic breakup, a serious illness, a child leaving home, a long-distance move—all these can trigger an overwhelming sense of loneliness.

At such times it helps me to remember that Jesus experienced loneliness deeper and more devastating than mine—and he understands how I feel. He had no spouse, no children, no true peers. And on the cross, when the world's sin separated him from God, Jesus' loneliness was so intense he cried out, "My God, my God, why have you forsaken me?" (Matt. 27:46).

Yet somehow the Son of God was made more perfect through the experience of suffering. According to Hebrews, "Even though Jesus was God's Son, he learned obedience from the things he suffered. In this way, God qualified him as a perfect High Priest, and he became the source of eternal salvation for all those who obey him" (Heb. 5:8-9).

Jesus learned obedience through suffering, and so must we. In our impatience and restlessness, we try to escape lonely moments rather than allow God to shape us in them. But as I've struggled to deal with my loneliness, I've come to realize that the "solution" doesn't lie in increased activity but in facing the reality of loneliness and seeking the presence of God within it.

My adopted daughter, Meagan, is more than a year old now. I'm no longer intensely lonely—I'm filled with Meagan's delicious smiles (and exhausted by her energy). Even so, she doesn't meet all my needs for affection and companionship.

> *God will not leave us alone—ever. He'll make us into what he created us to be.*
> YVONNE G. BAKER

But even in this season of relative fullness, I still benefit from the gift I've received from loneliness—I'm much more able to reach out to God.

As a Christian, I know nothing can separate me from the love of God. And I know suffering won't last forever. One day, Christ will return and all creation will be redeemed (Rom. 8:18-39). So while I long for the second coming of Christ, I cling to the promise of God's presence with me today. I may feel lonely, but I am never alone.

*Bonnie Budzowski*

11

# A Step Further

### Surviving Loneliness

1. *Reach out to God.* As you begin to seek God rather than the solutions he can provide, your relationship will deepen.
2. *Reach out to others.* Christian friends and family can provide much-needed prayer and love during your lonely season. And others experiencing pain similar to yours can provide a network of companionship and support.
3. *Be honest with God.* Take your pain to God in prayer. Though your problem may not be immediately solved, you'll experience God's presence.
4. *Submit your current circumstances to God.* Is there something specific God wants you to be doing while your dreams are on hold? Allow him to work through your brokenness—you may be surprised by the rich rewards.                    BB

## Faith Focus

At what times in your life have you felt lonely? Are you currently going through such a time? What benefits do you see from such times in the past—what have you learned? how have your friendships or your view of God changed?

### *Prayer Pointer*

Be honest with God about your lonely times. Ask him to help you submit all your circumstances to his guidance and care and to give you a deep sense of his presence. Thank Jesus for being your omnipresent friend—and for never leaving you alone.

Teach me your ways, O Lord, that I may live according to your truth! Grant me purity of heart, that I may honor you. With all my heart I will praise you, O Lord my God. I will give glory to your name forever.

Psalm 86:11-12

*H*ave you ever watched a movie where unbelievable things happen? For instance, on a single day a woman is kidnapped by foreign terrorists, defuses a bomb with a nail file and a credit card, and then is rescued by a blond hunk—just before she's hit by a drug lord's car.

Such events are so exaggerated that I'm glad my day is boring by comparison! However, when life is ho-hum it's tempting to add drama to our stories instead of living in truth (Ps. 86).

So here's the truth about exaggeration— and why we shouldn't fall into the trap.

# The Truth about Exaggeration

- "I have nothing to wear."

  Translation: *I haven't gone shopping for a while, and I don't feel like wearing the clothes I already own.*
- "My house is a total wreck."

  Translation: *The kitchen is cluttered, and I haven't vacuumed in a week.*

We've all exaggerated a story, dramatized a situation, or shaded the details to make our tale more horrific or gripping. We may do it for effect, to elicit sympathy and attention, or because we truly saw our situation in a more vivid light. Whatever the reason, many of us have cast ourselves in the role of heroine in a private drama played out in intense colors and powerful emotions.

Is exaggeration harmless, a colorful way to converse that helps us communicate more descriptively with others? Or can we hurt others and ourselves when we habitually embellish and dramatize? Might it even be a sin?

The embellishment trap is subtle because our motives are often benign. When we share with friends our struggles over our kids, weight, work, relationships, and homes, the commiseration can start to fly thick and fast.

Another reason we dramatize is because we think our lives lack excitement. It's an unconscious effort to add a little spice to the boring white bread of daily life.

But sometimes exaggeration signifies a deeper problem. Years ago, I had a friend who always had to top my story. If I was having a bad-hair day, she had a rare glandular condition that would render her bald. My friend was a funny and enjoyable companion. But because of a difficult childhood, she doubted her worth and felt compelled to present herself as a sort of soap-opera heroine. The sad irony was that in seeking others' approval through this behavior, she lost friends who grew tired of looking for the real woman under the embellishment.

Scripture reminds us to be truthful. My concordance lists dozens of entries for *true, truth,* and *truthful.* Solomon states it bluntly: "Truth stands the test of time; lies are soon exposed" (Prov. 12:19). All three of the apostle John's letters make frequent reference to walking in the truth. And the apostle James instructs us to "just say a simple yes or no, so that you will not sin and be condemned for it" (5:12).

> *God isn't impressed with sophisticated words, but with sincere hearts.*
>
> PAMELA PEARSON WONG AND KELSEY D. MENEHAN

The Bible clearly implies that those of us who have received the Truth—in the form of Jesus Christ—should seek to model truth in our daily lives. If we habitually, consciously embroider the truth, we hurt others because we deny them the chance to know the real person behind our exaggerated stories. We risk alienating them because we're forever hogging the limelight with our soap-opera anecdotes. And we hurt ourselves because we may start believing our own fabrications.

You're an interesting person—just as you are! People would like to get to know you: the real you, unadorned. Why not let them see it?     *Elizabeth Cody Newenhuyse*

# A Step Further

## Telling the Truth

1. *Check your conversations.* Listen to yourself talk. If you're caught in the trap of shading the facts, admit to yourself and to God that you're doing it.
2. *Think before you speak.* Before you say it, ask yourself: *Could this hurt someone? Could it help someone? Is it accurate?*
3. *Check your motive.* If you find yourself hiding behind a curtain of exaggeration, ask why you can't just be yourself. We all have qualities we don't feel good about. But people are powerfully drawn to someone who is real—just as God made her.
4. *Analyze your life.* Is boredom leading you to embellish everything? You may need to make a change—get more involved at church, find a new job, start an exercise program.          ECN

## Faith Focus

Do you tend to exaggerate? What would your friends say about you if they were asked the same question? If you do exaggerate, why do you do it—do you seek approval, better self-esteem, or a more exciting life? In what areas do you need to start telling the absolute truth today?

### Prayer Pointer

Thank God that he is holy, pure, and absolutely truthful. Ask him to help you tell "just the facts" when you open your mouth. Pray that our Lord will give you the courage to walk away from the temptation of embellishing the truth.

THERE IS ONLY ONE GOD AND FATHER, WHO IS OVER US ALL AND IN US ALL AND LIVING THROUGH US ALL. HOWEVER, HE HAS GIVEN EACH ONE OF US A SPECIAL GIFT ACCORDING TO THE GENEROSITY OF CHRIST.

EPHESIANS 4:6-7

*I*s a silk plant the only kind you can keep alive? Do you wonder how the full-time working mom next door manages to keep a spotless house while you struggle to dust once a month? Do you wish you could entertain as effortlessly as your friend? Do you dream about the day when you will be able to cook more than canned ravioli?

You may not be Suzy Homemaker, but that's OK. We're all created by God with special gifts, as Ephesians 4 says above. So here's how you can have your very own "Home Beautiful"—uniquely suited to you!

# Home Beautiful

I used to think only a few people really possess the gift of creative decorating. I was equally certain I wasn't one of them. After all, my kitchen cabinets hold more plastic action-figure cups than lovely goblets.

For a long time, I explained away my neighbor Sally's natural ability for creating beauty on the fact that she stayed home and had only one child. My house would look like that, too, I reasoned, if I didn't have two children and a job!

But then Sally opened a day care in her home and had six kids in her house every day. This I had to see! So, measuring cup in hand, I headed to Sally's to borrow some sugar. Hanging on her front door was a cute little blackboard with a Memo to Parents: Today's Lunch—homemade vegetable soup, orange-slice smiles, and whole-wheat crackers. Today's Snack—peanut-butter-and-jelly stars!

"Cute sign," I commented when Sally opened the door. "I just need a cup of sugar. I'm making . . . uh, clown-shaped snickerdoodle cookies for the girls."

I looked around but didn't see any children—or their mess. "What happened to the kids?"

"They're in the playroom. Go see what I did in there."

I went down the hall and looked in. It wasn't a room; it was a park. Sally had painted an outdoor motif on the walls, complete with sky, puffy clouds, grass, and trees. Little white park benches perched against two walls. Next to the silk tree sat a picnic table covered in a red-and-white checkered plastic tablecloth.

"It's beautiful in here, Sally. But I bet the kids can really make a mess of it, huh?"

"Oh, they know the rules: 'Put away before you play,'" she replied.

I couldn't take it anymore, so I asked her for some sugar, thanked her, and headed toward my house, the one with the crooked curtains and red stain on the dining-room carpet. The girls were playing with Lincoln Logs and Barbies . . . in the kitchen.

With a deep sigh I said to my husband, "Honey, I think I'll move in with Sally."

"No, you can't," he said with a teasing grin. "Who would clean up this mess?"

> *If you're a child of God, there's no room*
> *to envy someone else's gifts.*
> BODIE THOENE

After living next to Sally for eleven years, I'm finally learning I can't be Sally, or Martha Stewart, or anyone else for that matter. I agree with author Primo Levi, who wrote, "I live in my house as I live inside my skin; I know more beautiful, more ample, more sturdy, and more picturesque skins; but it would seem to me unnatural to exchange them for mine." I think maybe I do have what it takes to create beauty. It's just that I have to be more comfortable with my own style.

This realization called for celebration. So I poured red punch into four plastic Batman cups. My family and I raised our glasses and toasted who we are in Christ, and I reveled in the miracle of this "home beautiful." *Marsha Crockett*

# A STEP FURTHER

### What's Your Entertaining Style?

1. *Define what* home *means to you.* Is it a quiet haven in which to recharge or a place where others zoom in and out?
2. *Decide what "look" you're comfortable with.* No matter your style (contemporary, homespun, or Victorian), keep your menu and decorations simple.
3. *Look at your personality.* Are you spontaneous, or do you prefer planned activities? Adjust your hostess schedule accordingly.
4. *Decide how to involve your guests.* Will you allow them to bring a portion of the meal? a favorite game?
5. *Evaluate a "successful" evening.* Does it mean the food was delicious, your table beautiful—or that your guests were comfortable? Remember that success depends, in the long run, on whether your guests would want to come back. RCT

## Faith Focus

Look around your home—whether it's an apartment, townhouse, dorm, condo, or single-family dwelling. How does it reflect you and your unique, God-given gifts? In what ways could you use your "home beautiful" to befriend others and make an eternal impact for God's kingdom?

### Prayer Pointer

Thank God for your "home beautiful" and the many other blessings he's poured into your life. Ask him to turn your thoughts away from who others are to who he's gifted you to be. Then ask him to show you ways to make your home even more useful for his purposes.

I WILL THANK YOU, LORD, WITH ALL MY HEART; I WILL TELL OF ALL THE MARVELOUS THINGS YOU HAVE DONE. I WILL BE FILLED WITH JOY BECAUSE OF YOU. I WILL SING PRAISES TO YOUR NAME, O MOST HIGH.

PSALM 9:1-2

*D*oing laundry. Brushing your teeth. Driving to work. Washing the dishes. Making dinner. Grocery shopping.

Much of life is so, well, *ordinary*. When we think of what we spend most of our days doing, it's all some of us can do to stifle a yawn. Yet when we look back on the past, even the ordinary moments weave part of the rich tapestry of who we are and who we're becoming. If you're sometimes bored with life, here's how to transform the ho-hum into the hip, hip, hooray!

# The Splendor of the Ordinary

We'd anticipated the celebration for weeks. The morning dawned crisp, cool, and sunny—custom-made for "Pomp and Circumstance." I was the typical mother who reached for Kleenex as the maroon-and-white procession started down the aisle, and I suddenly realized a little girl is grown.

Our row of chairs was filled with aunts, uncles, cousins, and grandparents. We laughed, cried, and stretched high in our seats to see over the heads to the only face in the crowd that mattered—our graduate. We proudly clicked our cameras, waved our programs, and smiled from ear to ear. It was a moment to be captured and enshrined forever.

The party actually had started three days earlier when the first out-of-town relative arrived at the airport. The house was spotless, the refrigerator filled with a grand assortment of food. Gifts arrived in the mail, phone calls came from relatives in distant states, and friends and neighbors dropped in to add their congratulations. It was a jubilant time—like few others we had known.

I wanted to stop the clock. But all too soon we were making the return trip to the airport, waving good-bye, cleaning up the crumbs under the dining-room table, and throwing away the wrinkled bows and wrapping paper. I washed the last dish, watched the video of the graduation ceremony for one last time and suddenly life was ordinary again. I fed the cat, watered my geraniums on the front porch, then sat down and grieved for the high schooler I no longer had and for the celebration that was no more.

Life contains emotional peaks where we wish we could sit forever. We would much rather celebrate than clean out the garage or wash dirty dishes. But life hands us unadorned days filled with functional routine. Staleness threatens, like the dull, dry days of August when the air conditioner hums all day, the Kool-Aid keeps disappearing from the refrigerator, and the mailman brings nothing but pizza coupons and a sale flyer from the hardware store.

Most mornings, we do not jump enthusiastically out of bed to exciting, action-packed moments. Rather, we put one foot in front of the other and do what needs to be done—making breakfast, going to work, doing laundry, weeding the flower beds, answering correspondence, paying bills. Nondescript days. Ordinary moments. Life can easily reduce itself to boredom unless we know how to wrap ordinary moments with fresh meaning and purpose.

*Thanking God helps me focus on blessings I can so easily take for granted—things like food to eat, a bed to sleep in, and family and friends who love me. What are you thankful for today?*
ELIZABETH MITTELSTAEDT

So how does one go about transforming ordinary moments into meaningful celebrations of life? The place to begin is to accept the fact that most of life is ordinary. For a day is not ordinary or extraordinary in itself. It is ordinary or extraordinary depending on how I view it and what I choose to do with it. Given in joyful abandonment, ordinary moments become stepping-stones to growth and discovery—in every area of our life, including our relationship with God!

*Ruth Senter*

# A Step Further

## Hunting for Splendor

1. *Live today well.* An old Indian motto is, "Every yesterday is a dream of happiness; every tomorrow is a vision of hope. And every today can be well lived."

2. *Develop your powers of observation.* Feel the wind in your face as you take your walk; note the crab-apple blossoms; listen for God's gentle whisper.

3. *Look for the surprising and unpredictable.* "If you look for me in earnest, you will find me when you seek me" (Jer. 29:13). If we want to see God in the ordinary moments of our day, we must always be examining, expecting, reflecting. The Lord Jesus Christ came in a way no one expected.

4. *Learn to be flexible.* Schedules, as useful as they are, may well be God's greatest obstacle when he seeks our attention.

RS

**Faith Focus**

How do you treat your ordinary moments? Do you see them as special or as something you merely have to get through? In what ways can you celebrate today's ordinary moments?

## Prayer Pointer

Ask God to help you think of each moment of your day as special. Ask him to help you redeem your time—even the unexpected or dull moments—for his good purposes. Thank God for knowing you intimately and loving you!

I AM CONVINCED THAT NOTHING CAN EVER SEPARATE US FROM HIS LOVE. DEATH CAN'T, AND LIFE CAN'T. THE ANGELS CAN'T, AND THE DEMONS CAN'T. OUR FEARS FOR TODAY, OUR WORRIES ABOUT TOMORROW, AND EVEN THE POWERS OF HELL CAN'T KEEP GOD'S LOVE AWAY.

ROMANS 8:38

- If only I hadn't opened my mouth.
- If only I hadn't met him at a time in my life when I didn't feel good about myself.
- If only I'd had more supportive parents.

Who hasn't been haunted by "if onlys"? They can become so overwhelming that they strip the joy from life. But Scripture gives an antidote in Romans 8:38. We need not worry about past, present, *or* future because nothing keeps God's love away! There are ways to stop second-guessing your past—and start living.

# If Only I Had . . .

If God allowed second chances in life, what would you do differently? My mom says she would spend less time housekeeping and more time playing with her children. Other women tell me they would say no to premarital sex, marry someone else, or not marry at all. I would probably rewrite my entire career.

When life gets tough—when our dreams don't come true exactly as planned—we often blame ourselves and second-guess what might have been if only we'd made a different choice or behaved differently. Our disappointment may start out as a healthy hunger for something better, but the moment we question God's promises, our disappointment turns into doubt, producing an unhealthy lack of faith we call regret.

To regret is to sling mud at life's big picture; our present sufferings and disappointments seem more real and important than the glory God promises to reveal in us someday (see Rom. 8:18, 28).

Do you remember what happened to Lot's wife when she looked back as her family fled from Sodom? She became a pillar of salt (Gen. 19:26). Stone-faced. Immobile. Useless to anyone. If we don't learn from our mistakes and move on, we too can become useless to God.

One day, Proverbs 20:5 caught my attention. "Though good advice lies deep within a person's heart, the wise will draw it out," Solomon wrote. God was telling me to examine my motives. On the surface, they were commendable. But when I looked deeper, I found my regret was rooted in the sin of pride and an inordinate desire to project a glamorous image.

I prayed, *You're right, Lord. I wanted glory for me, not you. I wanted to feel good about myself, but now I see I was looking for fulfillment in the wrong place.*

Like any of God's promises, forgiveness depends on faith, not feelings. Too often we expect our sorrow to lift like a cloud, our regret to dissipate like vapor. The truth is, regret goes away according to the measure of our faith in God and our understanding of his character.

> *There will be many times in your life when you feel like running away. These moments can crush or strengthen you—you alone can choose.*
>
> SHEILA WALSH

At some point we have to stop punishing ourselves for being human and for living in an imperfect world in which Satan is actively trying to destroy us. Disappointment and tragedy are real, but so is our God. He will never leave us nor forsake us, no matter what (Deut. 31:6). Not even our bad decisions or inactions can separate us from the love of God (Rom. 8:39).

Store these Scriptures in your heart, and there won't be any room for regret. Start believing God and giving thanks to him for all things, for you can be joyful even in a bad marriage, job situation, or living arrangement. Set your hearts on the process of growth, and you won't ever want to turn back the clock again.  *Michele Halseide*

# A Step Further

### Routing Regret from Your Life

1. *Get to the heart of the problem.* When you hear yourself saying, "If only I had . . . ," stop and identify the real source of your disappointment. Is it guilt over unconfessed sin? Choose to confess and receive Christ's forgiveness.
2. *Praise without ceasing.* We can be thankful for any experience that exercises our faith and teaches us how to persevere. Dealing with adversity is what gives our Christian walk depth and authenticity. Thank God for this truth.
3. *Bloom where you're planted.* Choose to make the best of the situation. When you dwell on regrets, you inhibit growth.
4. *Trust in God's providence.* God guides all human destiny. We can plan our lives in great detail, but the Lord's purpose will always prevail (Prov. 19:21).   MH

## Faith Focus

Is there anything you regret about your life (an action you carried out or something that was done to you)? How have you dealt with the aftereffects of this "if only"? Which of the four steps for routing regret from your life will you choose to start today?

### Prayer Pointer

Pour out the situation(s) you regret before the Lord, who understands you better than anyone else. Ask him for his help in giving this "if only" over to him—and not taking it back. Thank him for being a God who answers prayer.

For all of God's promises have been fulfilled in him. That is why we say "Amen" when we give glory to God through Christ. It is God who gives us, along with you, the ability to stand firm for Christ.

2 Corinthians 1:20-21

$\mathcal{G}$ood intentions. In today's busy world it's easy to say—and mean—

- I'll give you a call.
- I'll pray for you.
- The check's in the mail.
- Let's do lunch.
- Sure, I'll do that. Count me in!

But do we always follow through on our quick promises? Unfortunately, I don't. But God always does, according to 2 Corinthians 1:20. And if we want to grow closer to God, we must commit to keeping our promises too. Following are some ideas on how we can make good on our good intentions.

# Promises, Promises . . .

A while back, I chatted with a woman at a school event, someone I'd crossed paths with for years and often thought I'd like to get to know better. As we ended our conversation, I said, "Let's get together for coffee as soon as I'm out from under the pile."

"I'd like that," she said.

Well, I've been out from under that particular pile for two years—but I've never called her.

Why is it so easy to toss off promises as lightly as we drop a tissue into a wastebasket? We say: "I'll write you"; "I'll call"; "Let's have lunch"; "I'll be sure to pray about that." Sometimes we deliver. Sometimes we don't.

Too often "I'll call you" really means "See you later." It's become a glib social shorthand everyone understands. We don't really intend to follow up; it's just that we're caught up in warm feelings and lively conversation at a party, a business function, or coffee hour after church, and we commit to something that's weeks or months in the future. Then time passes, and life gets in the way, and more time passes. . . .

On a scale of bad behavior, not phoning someone when you say you will seems like a minor, forgivable trespass. It isn't as if you're lying, cheating, or stealing. But a pattern of unkept commitments—or even one big broken promise—can damage a relationship. And God cares about our relationships with others, both believers and unbelievers, because he wants us to reflect him in those relationships: "And whatever you do or say, let it be as a representative of the Lord Jesus, all the while giving thanks through him to God the Father" (Col. 3:17).

I once heard about a couple I'd call "seekers" who visited a church and received warm promises from the pastor and deacons that they would call or come by. No one called, no one visited. The incident left the couple feeling soured on church and Christians in general.

And throughout Scripture, from Proverbs to James, there are warnings against the harm a loose tongue can do. The apostle James goes as far as to call the tongue "an uncontrollable evil, full of deadly poison" (3:8).

*God keeps his promises—so we should, too.*
MAYO MATHERS

Our promises matter to God, who holds us to a different standard. In the words of a sermon I heard recently, "God wants our thoughts to be like his thoughts." Our God is a God of covenants, the Lord who throughout Scripture keeps his promises—to Noah, to Abraham, to Jacob and Moses, to David, and on down to the ultimate promise fulfilled in Christ. He promises to be with us always, and he delivers.

Out of love and obedience to our covenant-keeping God, we should commit our speech and actions to him, asking for wisdom and discernment in all the commitments we make. Christ wants his glory to be reflected in us and will equip us for every challenge. And that's a promise that will never be broken.

*Elizabeth Cody Newenhuyse*

# A STEP FURTHER

## Be a Promise Keeper

1. *Watch what you say*. Don't commit to something out of well-meaning impulsiveness. Make specific promises only when you know you can keep them.
2. *Sleep on it*. Ask for a day or more to think over a potential commitment. That way, you're not swayed by pressure from others or the spirit of the moment.
3. *Know when to say no*. There are only so many ways you can use your talents and so many hours in a day. When you've reached your limit, don't commit to anything more. People will appreciate an honest *no* more than an unfulfilled *yes*.
4. *Just do it*. Know what works for you. Do you need to write commitments in your Day-Timer, on strategically placed Post-its, or on your to-do list? ECN

## Faith Focus

Do you always make good on your good intentions? When's the last time you've kept—or broken—even a quick promise? Which of the "promise keeper" steps will you incorporate the next time you open your mouth to respond with a promise?

### Prayer Pointer

Thank the Lord for recording his promises to us in the Bible. Praise him for never breaking his promises to you. Then ask him to help you become a woman after his own heart, someone who always makes good on her good intentions.

ALL OF US HAVE HAD THAT VEIL REMOVED SO THAT WE CAN BE MIRRORS THAT BRIGHTLY REFLECT THE GLORY OF THE LORD. AND AS THE SPIRIT OF THE LORD WORKS WITHIN US, WE BECOME MORE AND MORE LIKE HIM AND REFLECT HIS GLORY EVEN MORE.

2 CORINTHIANS 3:18

*I* first met Joani as a college sophomore and avoided her wherever possible. Although she was friendly, her habits drove me crazy. She interrupted conversations to throw in her "top it all" stories. She always knew best how to tackle a project. And she could top any term-paper research with an omniscient comment. After a while, no one wanted to hang out with Joani; she was a well-known know-it-all.

If you wish at times you had a better control on your lips, here's some practical help from a self-professed but now reformed know-it-all.

# The Day I Kept My Mouth Shut

I was surprised to hear Elisabeth Elliot Gren on a recent radio broadcast advise listeners, "Never pass up an opportunity to keep your mouth shut." Her advice obviously was directed at those of us with an answer for everything, so I decided to see what would happen when I zipped my lips.

Not long after, I attended a Bible study about spiritual gifts at my friend Ellen's house. In the middle of our conversation, Linda, one of the members, interrupted with a question: "When I was in college, I ran out of money. I prayed, and a few days later my mother sent me a check for fifty dollars. In her letter, Mom said she sensed I had a financial need. Since she wasn't a Christian, could she still have been used by God?"

I immediately thought of the Old Testament passage in Numbers 22 where Balaam's donkey kept him out of the path of an opposing angel—proving God can use anybody or anything to accomplish his work. I was ready to rush in with my words of wisdom—until *Never pass up an opportunity to keep your mouth shut* flitted through my mind.

A few minutes later, Linda said quietly, "I just remembered how God used Balaam's donkey."

The other women laughed and agreed with Linda's observation while my mouth flew open in surprise. I learned then that although God has used some unlikely objects in the past, he really doesn't need *my* big mouth to get his work done.

Later I wondered how Linda would have reacted if *I'd* been the one to compare her mother to a donkey. I'm glad I kept my mouth shut!

Next came the really big test—my husband! Al and I had been married two years. I'm a neatnik, and Al is . . . a lot more laid-back than I am. I'd lectured him since our wedding day about leaving clothes and magazines lying around.

Al's response? He ignored me. Occasionally, when I'd act really angry, he'd pick up his things. Then he'd leave for work, and I'd be stuck with this funny guilty feeling. So I decided to try keeping quiet with Al.

The next morning, without saying a word, I picked up his dirty clothes from the bathroom floor and put them in the hamper. It was sort of fun. I imagined myself as a servant—the type the Bible mentions—and that made me feel good. I noticed an absence of the guilty feeling as Al kissed me tenderly before leaving for work.

> *Our world is full of talk but short on sensitive,*
> *wise, gentle listeners.*
> VINITA HAMPTON WRIGHT

A few weeks later, as I continued keeping quiet (and picking up his things), I began to notice a change in Al. He did yard work with eagerness and gladly helped me sand some old chairs. But more than that, his whole attitude toward me changed. There was a new sweetness in our relationship, a deeper feeling of love. He even began to pick up his clothes.

And all I had to do was keep quiet. You may want to try it!

*Mary Roberts Clark*

# A Step Further

## Help for Zipping Your Lips

1. *Don't give advice—unless it's asked for.*
   Then be gentle, not forceful in your
   opinion. This is the number one advice
   from mothers-in-law and daughters-in-
   law who have a good relationship.
2. *Do watch and listen before you open
   your mouth.* It's amazing what you can
   discover *before* you stick your foot in
   your mouth!
3. *Don't criticize.* Just because someone
   doesn't do a task the way you do, it
   doesn't mean they're doing it wrong.
4. *Don't say, "I told you . . .";* do say, "I
   love you . . . and I appreciate you."* Many
   of life's relational problems could be
   solved with this simple rule.        RCT

## Faith Focus

How often do you "pass up an opportunity to keep your mouth shut"? Would any of the ideas from "How to Zip Your Lips" be helpful for you to consider? The next time you have an opportunity to share your opinion unnecessarily, what will you choose to do?

### Prayer Pointer

Thank God for loving you enough to point out the times when you are wrong. Ask him to help you know when you should be silent and when you should speak. Thank him in advance for his assistance.

There is a time for everything, a season for every activity under heaven. A time to be born and a time to die. A time to plant and a time to harvest. A time to kill and a time to heal. A time to tear down and a time to rebuild. A time to cry and a time to laugh. A time to grieve and a time to dance.

ECCLESIASTES 3:1-4

*W*hen do tears get ahold of you—after a hectic workday, after an awful scene with your teenager, when a loved one is injured or dies, when you're disappointed in yourself or a friend?

Some of us find it difficult to express sorrow because we wonder if it's "Christian" to weep. But as the writer of Ecclesiastes says, sorrow is a part of life—there's "a time to cry" and "a time to grieve." So the next time the need for a good cry sneaks up on you, don't be afraid to let the tears roll.

# The Power of a Good Cry

It was a bad Monday. I'd just started a new job, and I was exhausted with all the mental energy of remembering people's names, absorbing the technicalities of a different computer system, and trying to make heads or tails out of new procedures.

When I arrived home and walked in my kitchen door, I immediately shed my shoes and jacket with a sigh of relief. But the relief was short-lived. In the next instant, I slid across the floor in a gooey puddle of chocolate ice cream.

*What on earth?* I thought, dazed. Then I looked down and saw the spoon. Evidently our young live-in guest had once again decided to plop on the kitchen floor and read while she had a snack and had forgotten to put the rest away. So there it was—the entire half-gallon of soupy mess.

As I stood there, angry thoughts swirling through my brain and nylons sticking to the floor, I noticed something else. Only *one* of my parakeets was sitting on her perch. When I looked closer, the other one was lying stiff— dead—on the bottom of the cage.

Overwhelmed, ticked, and sad, I didn't know which emotion to tackle first. So I did what solved all of them—I plopped on the floor and had myself a good cry!

That day I realized how powerful a good cry is. For me, it was like a cleanser, scrubbing away all the awful happenings of the day. It took care of the tenseness in my stomach and the ache in my head over my workday. It swept away my anger about the ice cream needlessly left melting on the floor. It helped to soothe my sadness over losing a pet I'd had for more than eight years. Those cleansing tears freed me to begin thinking positively about how to problem-solve the situation with our live-in guest rather than dwelling on revenge.

Perhaps that's why the Scriptures are peppered with references to mourning or crying that ends up as rejoicing. Jeremiah 31:13 says: "I will turn their mourning into joy. I will comfort them and exchange their sorrow for rejoicing." And Isaiah proclaims, "Those who have been ransomed by the Lord will return to Jerusalem, singing songs of everlasting joy. Sorrow and mourning will disappear, and they will be overcome with joy and gladness" (35:10).

*God says he will give you beauty for ashes, joy for mourning, and a garment of praise for the spirit of despair. The only requirement is a willingness to relinquish control of your life to God.*

MARY WHELCHEL

When you think Christians shouldn't cry because they're not showing a victorious spirit, remember that even Jesus felt great sadness during his days on earth. At the grave of Lazarus, he wept (see John 11:35).

So when you've had a tough day, don't be afraid to use God's release valve—the power of a healing cry. It'll help you and others around you. (*Psychology Today* reported that those who take time to cry are less likely to take their emotions out on others.) So go ahead and cry—it's good for you!                              *Ramona Cramer Tucker*

# A Step Further

### Go Ahead—Let the Tears Flow!

1. *Watch a good movie.* Many classics have heartrending scenes. So don't be afraid to get out the tissues and sniffle away!
2. *Get away by yourself during hormonal swings.* Even if you're just taking a five-minute walk, a short cry will give you more emotional balance in front of your loved ones.
3. *Don't apologize for your tears.* Even young children can understand tears if you say, "Mommy is just sad right now. But crying helps it to be OK, so don't worry."
4. *Realize tears are for joyful times, too.* For instance, the adoption of a baby, a wedding, good news about a friend's health.
5. *Don't be afraid of being vulnerable.* But also be careful not to *use* your tears to manipulate others to do what you want.

RCT

## Faith Focus

How often do you cry—and when? What do you think when you see others cry (do you see it as embarrassing, necessary, comforting, etc.)? In order to have a balanced emotional life, do you need to try any of the tips under "Go Ahead—Let the Tears Flow!"?

### Prayer Pointer

Thank God for sending Jesus Christ to earth in human form so he can understand *all* our emotions. Ask God to help you learn when it's appropriate—and not appropriate—to cry. Thank him for creating you with your unique emotional makeup.

I AM HOLDING YOU BY YOUR RIGHT HAND—I, THE LORD YOUR GOD. AND I SAY TO YOU, "DO NOT BE AFRAID. I AM HERE TO HELP YOU." AND THE JOY OF THE LORD WILL FILL YOU TO OVERFLOWING.

ISAIAH 41:13, 16

*W*hat do you fear? That a loved one will get hurt, become ill, or die? That your car won't start on a wintry day? That you'll make a fool of yourself during your big presentation? That you'll never get out of your dead-end job?

Fear can paralyze us if we let it. But Scripture gives us the way out in Isaiah 41: it says we need not be afraid because God himself will help us—and fill us with joy instead.

With God's help, here's how we can face fear head-on and transform it into greater faith.

# Transforming Fear into Faith

For most of my life, I was controlled by fear. At times, I worried about disasters that might happen to my loved ones. I feared losing control and panicked at the thought of disappointing people or facing rejection.

The more I talked to other women, the more I knew I wasn't alone. Once I began writing books, I started getting letters from women all across the country who wrote to me about their fears. Many women are afraid of getting trapped in a dead-end life. Others are afraid of failing to balance their work and home life.

Most of us believe that faith in Christ brings contentment, peace, and joy. So when we still experience fear, we feel like a spiritual failure!

I experienced huge fear during the first year of our marriage when I was in a devastating car accident that threatened to ruin us financially. While driving to work in rush-hour traffic, my car's accelerator stuck. In my frantic attempts to get the car stopped, it never occurred to me to simply turn off the ignition!

My car ended up hitting four vehicles and pulling out a fire hydrant and a park bench before it rammed into the plate-glass window of the IBM building in downtown Grand Rapids. Fortunately, I'd jumped out before that happened and no one was seriously injured, but the next day we found out that because of a mistake made by a previous employer, we weren't insured.

There my husband, Gene, and I were, twenty-two years old, facing tremendous financial problems. I was terrified that we'd never be able to afford a home or family of our own. And I was embarrassed to admit to anyone that I thought God had let me down. But in my heart, I just cried out, *Why, God? This is so unfair!*

For a time, I was held up by my husband's faith. I recall the day Gene took my hands in his and prayed, "Lord, we don't understand why we're wiped out financially. But we know you're God, and nothing can touch us without your permission. Right now we affirm our belief that you can turn this to good; even if in this lifetime we don't understand why you've allowed us to go through this, we still choose to trust you."

> *If you allow God to make you into the person he has in mind, what do you have to fear of the future? You are his daughter.*
> DOROTHY ARMSTRONG

At that moment, I don't think I could quite believe what Gene was saying. But God used it to minister to me. I thought of Philippians 4:6: "Don't worry about anything; instead, pray about everything. Tell God what you need, and thank him for all he has done."

I began to realize there were some things to be thankful for. Nobody had been killed in the accident. After several legal battles, the judge determined I wasn't liable for additional damages. Finally, when I saw what God had spared me from, I was able to rejoice and say, "God, you did some pretty incredible things that day!"
*Carol Kent
with Jan L. Senn*

# A STEP FURTHER

### Getting the Jump on Fear

1. *Realize that some fear is positive.* All believers should have a holy fear of our awesome God. And self-preserving fear makes you run from danger—it's God's way of protecting you.

2. *Develop an eternal perspective.* Remember that even in the middle of your difficult situation, God is still in control of the universe.

3. *Stop relying on your strength.* Surrendering your will to God's and choosing to trust him allows you to begin making faith-filled decisions.

4. *Take a step of faith.* Make that phone call or sign up for that class. Putting your faith into action helps you move past fear. CK with JLS

## Faith Focus

What things do you fear? Have those fears in any way kept you from acting in a particular situation? Which of the four suggestions in "Getting the Jump on Fear" can you apply today to begin to transform that fear into a greater faith?

### *Prayer Pointer*

Tell God your fears—he can handle them. Thank him for being a great, awesome God who walks beside you through every situation, even the most fearsome. Ask him to help you trust him more.

Since we are receiving a kingdom that cannot be destroyed, let us be thankful and please God by worshiping him with holy fear and awe. For our God is a consuming fire.

Hebrews 12:28-29

DAY 11

$\mathcal{D}$o you agree to do a project you hate so that others will like and include you? How much of your time do you spend working hard in order to please others, including your family, church, and community? Does it bother you when you're not sure what others think of you?

All of us, to some extent, are people pleasers. It's only human to want others to like us. But Scriptures such as Hebrews 12 tell us that we should worship only God, never other people. Are you a people pleaser or a God pleaser? Here's how to find out.

# People Pleaser or God Pleaser?

I'm a people pleaser. I work overtime to please, impress, and placate friends and strangers because I need their affirmation to feel good about myself—especially my appearance.

Somehow an unhealthy self-consciousness has oozed into every area of my life, affecting how I spend my time and money, how I raise my children and set my priorities, even how I relate to other people.

I'm not alone, however. Many women I meet are people pleasers in one way or another. Take Jan, for instance. She overprepares for routine meetings because she always wants to appear competent. And Amanda won't invite a neighbor into her home unless it's spotless.

People pleasers are easily conned into competing for worthless accolades—often running ourselves into the ground in the process. We judge ourselves by others' standards and reel with pain when we don't match up. We pass up opportunities to talk about Jesus because we're too afraid to risk failure.

But God is a jealous ruler who demands exclusive devotion to himself (Exod. 34:14; Deut. 4:24; Josh. 24:19). We arouse his jealousy when we make idols out of ordinary people and derive our significance from the praises of men (Ps. 78:58). As we get sidetracked trying to win approval, we load our schedules with activities that appear worthwhile but actually keep us from the very things God has prepared in advance for us to do (Eph. 2:10).

There is a better way to live, and Mary, Martha's sister, found it (Luke 10:38-42). She wasn't worried about pleasing houseguests; she didn't need their approval. Mary had one overriding priority: to sit at Jesus' feet, stare into his eyes, and listen to God's word.

David had the same passion. "One thing I ask of the Lord—the thing I seek most—is to live in the house of the Lord all the days of my life, delighting in the Lord's perfections and meditating in his Temple" (Ps. 27:4).

Mary and David understood that we are transformed in the presence of the Lord. That is why our quest for significance and approval begins—and ends—with God. We will never grow in our relationship with God if we don't have the gumption to become single-minded, bent on pleasing God—and God only.

*As a Christian, my goal is to become more sensitive to the right kind of pressure—the gentle promptings of the Lord who created me and offers me the strength I need to live a life that pleases him.*

JANIS LONG HARRIS

When my friend Mindy recognized that God was interested in her mind-set for Sunday worship, not her outfit, she relaxed the family dress code. "At first I was embarrassed that my sons weren't the best-dressed kids in Sunday school," Mindy says. "But that feeling soon went away, especially when I began to see how it changed our family."

I admit that I haven't completely conquered my fear of rejection, but it hasn't conquered me. Now when a neighbor knocks at my door—and I'm still in my bathrobe—I force myself to remember that when Jesus looks into my eyes, he sees the presence of God's Spirit. Not my eyelashes. And certainly not my pale complexion. *Michele Halseide*

# A STEP FURTHER

## Living for the Right Applause

1. *Discover the source of your insecurity.* Whenever you catch yourself saying or doing something to impress others, try to determine its cause. Are you afraid of rejection or failure? Is it low self-esteem or envy?

2. *Plan alternative responses.* Before you enter situations where you might be tempted to people-please, think of God-pleasing alternatives and specific Scriptures to support them.

3. *Stop judging others.* Learn to view people as God does, by looking at the inside. Many wonderful surprises await us when we learn to fix our attention on the heart, not the hair or figure or ability.

4. *Dwell upon truth.* Memorize Scriptures that lambaste the sources of your insecurities.                     MH

**Faith Focus**

Think about the past week. By your actions and thoughts, have you been living for God's applause—or people's applause? What can you do today to make pleasing God your priority?

*Prayer Pointer*

Ask God to reveal to you today the areas in which you're pleasing him and the areas in which you're striving to please others. Thank him for drawing you continually closer to him, and ask him to help you live only for *his* applause.

How can I know all the sins lurking in my heart? Cleanse me from these hidden faults. Keep me from deliberate sins! Don't let them control me. Then I will be free of guilt and innocent of great sin. May the words of my mouth and the thoughts of my heart be pleasing to you, O Lord, my rock and my redeemer.

PSALM 19:12-14

*W*hat do you say when you get frustrated, when life just isn't going your way or something bad happens? It might depend on whether you're alone or surrounded by a crowd. Either way, some not-so-nice words can slip—even if you don't mean them to.

Scripture is clear that what comes out of our mouth is what's in our heart and mind. If we want to please God, we need to stay away from sins like swearing. So if you struggle sometimes with foot-in-mouth disease, here's help from someone who's been there.

# Say WHAT?

Having spent the first twenty-seven years of my life away from God and immersed in the ways of the world, I developed a vocabulary some might call "colorful." When the Lord yanked me out of that pit fourteen years ago and placed me on the path of righteousness, one of the first obvious changes was my language. *Hooray!* I thought. *No more cussing a blue streak.*

Well . . . yes and no. No, improper adjectives don't slip out as effortlessly as exhaling. But when stress rears its ugly head, my once-tame tongue leaps from her cage like a tiger unleashed.

For example, one afternoon, with less than an hour to make a flight to Atlanta, I dashed into the house through our kitchen and promptly caught the cat's milk dish with my toe, launching liquid all over my freshly mopped floor and my new leather shoes.

This wasn't the first time I'd spilled the cat dish, just the worst time. At the top of my lungs I shouted, "That #$%&!@##! will have to go somewhere else!"

At that precise moment, the door to our downstairs bathroom opened and the face of our housepainter appeared, his eyes wide with shock.

I was more than a little wide-eyed myself. "Oh! No, no, not you! You're welcome to go . . . anywhere you like." Sheepishly, I waved in the direction of the milk puddle. "I was talking to the cat dish."

"Uh . . . sure, ma'am," he said, sliding past me as he hurried for the back door and certain safety.

Oh, dear.

I fell into a chair, deeply ashamed at my lack of control. What a wretched woman! I prayed for forgiveness, then sought out our housepainter and begged his pardon as well. Not only was it the right thing to do, it was the only thing to do: He's a member of our church.

A word of wisdom from Proverbs came to mind: "If you keep your mouth shut, you will stay out of trouble" (Prov. 21:23). I should have meditated on that verse *before* the catfish disaster. Even with my heartfelt apology, I couldn't undo the damage I'd done to my friendship with the housepainter. My sinful outburst could cause him to stumble, or even cast the shadow of doubt on my commitment to Christ.

*We have to integrate the principles of God's Word in everything we do—including the kind of people we hang out with, the places we go, and the language we use.*

BABBIE MASON

When #$%&!@##! comes out of my mouth, it would be easy to blame the media or movies. But the fault is solely mine. The solution also rests at my doorstep, and the strength to avoid cursing comes from the Lord as I vow to "take captive every thought to make it obedient to Christ" (2 Cor. 10:5, NIV). I'm so glad that when I confess my transgressions, God forgives them, even one as mean-spirited and immature as my struggle with pure speech. How encouraging to remember that "anyone who loves a pure heart and gracious speech is the king's friend" (Prov. 22:11).

*Liz Curtis Higgs*

# A Step Further

## Four Tongue Tamers

1. *Pray before you speak.* The habit of ungodly speech will not go away by itself. Continually ask the Lord to make you strong in this regard.
2. *Ask for forgiveness.* When you slip up, immediately ask for forgiveness from God—and anyone within earshot!
3. *Be prepared.* You probably know the situations that make you most vulnerable to verbal sins. Do whatever you can to avoid those environments, or find some healthier ways to release frustration—like jogging up and down a stairway or taking some deep breaths.
4. *Remember: Garbage in, garbage out.* One way to control what comes out of your mouth is to restrict what goes into your mind. Try to avoid TV shows and movies with off-color language.     LCH

## Faith Focus

Do you struggle with putting your foot in your mouth sometimes? If so, at what times is it most difficult for you to control your language? Which of the four tongue tamers would help you when you're next tempted to use unedifying language?

*Prayer Pointer*

Ask God to reveal to you any language that doesn't honor him. Request that he help you learn to control your tongue and develop good habits. Thank him for being a God who loves you so much that he wants everything about your life to be pure and honorable.

Dear friends, we are already
God's children, and we can't
even imagine what we will be
like when Christ returns.
But we do know that when he
comes we will be like him, for
we will see him as he really is.

1 John 3:2

*A* drunk driver totals your car. Your twins are born early, requiring an extended hospital stay. One day you're working at a job you love—the next day you're given a pink slip. You suffer from depression.

Sooner or later we all face tough times. But in the midst of our discouragement, God gives us hope in verses such as 1 John 3:2. He encourages us by revealing to us throughout the Bible that this present life isn't all we have. He's giving us a joyful eternity with him! Here's why long-term thinking is so important.

# Looking Forward to Someday

"File this, Francie, and make copies of this letter, would you?" I recently asked my secretary. "And would you please pull out the sofa bed one more time?"

"Are you serious? Again?"

"Again." With that, my face flushed and my eyes became damp. For the fourth time that day, I needed to be lifted out of my wheelchair and laid down. Once again I had to be undressed to readjust my corset; shallow breathing and a sky-rocketing blood pressure signaled something was either pinching, bruising, or poking my paralyzed body. Francie tissued away my tears and unfolded the office sofa bed.

As she examined my legs and hips for any telltale irritation, I stared vacantly at the ceiling. "Where do I go to resign from this stupid paralysis?"

Francie couldn't find anything wrong. She redressed me, hoisted me back into my wheelchair, then stepped back, awaiting my response.

I looked sheepish. "I'm tired of this. If I were you, I'd send me back for a new body." Francie shook her head and grinned. She's heard me say that scores of times. It's nothing new. At times, I hate my disability.

As Francie was about to leave, she paused and leaned against the door. "I bet you can't wait for the resurrection. You know, like Paul said somewhere, 'We groan, longing to be clothed with a heavenly dwelling.'"

My eyes dampened again, but this time they were tears of relief and hope. I tried to return to my dictation, but that verse stuck with me. *Yes, Lord,* I thought, *I do look forward to being whole, to having a body that will never know pain* or problems. But to be honest, what I really want is a new heart. A heart free of disappointment and resentment. A heart that doesn't want to quit.

I squeezed back my tears and dreamed what I've dreamed of a thousand times—the promise of the resurrection. A flood of other hopeful promises filled my mind. *When we see him we shall be like him. The perishable shall put on the imperishable. That which is sown in weakness will be raised in power.* I opened my eyes and said out loud with a smile, "Come quickly, Lord Jesus."

> *While you're suffering, you can't see the "why." It's only after the fact that you see that God makes true his promises—he works all things together for good.*
> JAN DRAVECKY

The resurrection promise is not a lifeless, cross-stitched pledge on a plaque. If only we would allow suffering to get us ready for the hereafter, if only we would permit it to prepare us to meet God, then the hope of complete spiritual, emotional, mental, and physical resurrection would throb with vibrancy. Our strong desire for the imperishable would make the hereafter very real. Then Hebrews 12:22-23 would shine with that present-tense excitement: "You have come to Mount Zion, to the city of the living God, the heavenly Jerusalem, and to thousands of angels in joyful assembly. You have come to the assembly of God's firstborn children, whose names are written in heaven. You have come to God himself."                              *Joni Eareckson Tada*

# A Step Further

## The Benefits of Suffering

1. *Suffering gets us ready for the resurrection.*
   Broken necks, broken homes, and
   broken hearts crush our hopes that
   earthly things can satisfy. Only the
   promise of the resurrection—the
   glorious day when we will be whole—
   can truly move our eyes from this world.

2. *Suffering prepares us to meet God.*
   Suppose you never knew pain. No sore
   back, stained reputation, or bruised
   feelings. How could you appreciate the
   scarred hands with which Christ will
   greet you?

3. *Loyalty in suffering gives you something
   to offer Christ in return.* What other
   proof could you bring of your love and
   faithfulness if this life left you totally
   unscarred?                          JET

## Faith Focus

At what periods in your life have you suffered? What has God taught you in those trying times? In what ways will you choose to respond in the future when trials come your way?

### Prayer Pointer

Thank God for his mighty power and help in all situations, no matter how difficult. Thank him specifically for ways he's helped you through tough times in the past. Pray for strength to respond to future trials in a godly manner.

Don't get tired of doing what is good. Don't get discouraged and give up, for we will reap a harvest of blessing at the appropriate time. Whenever we have the opportunity, we should do good to everyone, especially to our Christian brothers and sisters.

Galatians 6:9-10

*W*hat does *hospitality* mean to you? Do you have visions of being a relaxed, well-dressed hostess who glides to the front door to greet her guests? Meanwhile, your table is lavishly laid with china, silver, and gourmet foods?

Well, I think if I—or my table—ever looked like that, I'd fall over in shock. The truth is, the difference between entertaining and hospitality is that entertaining has to be planned. Hospitality just happens in the regular course of life as we "do good to everyone."

Hospitality isn't as difficult as you might think.

# No Time to Entertain?

My friend's voice on the other end of the line was strained. Words poured out in a rush.

"I didn't know who to call. I'm scared! My neighbor's children have to be hidden from their father for their own safety. We've got to move quickly! Can I bring them over to your house right now?"

Somehow it wasn't supposed to be like this. Lounging in the serenity of my hospital bed the night before, I had envisioned my son's homecoming filled with the joys only a newborn can bring. I had imagined our family lying on the big bed together examining Andy's fingers and toes.

Now this. Serve as a house of safety for a family in trouble? Not in my plan! Yet the moment was now; the need was immediate.

Sometimes our call to be hospitable may come as a surprise. Yet our hectic lives fight against this sort of open-armed welcome. After all, we're already struggling valiantly to juggle homes and careers, children's science projects, and the report due on the boss's desk.

The world of entertaining comes with a list of expectations that stop us in our tracks, yet we live in a world of plastic tablecloths and Ground Beef Delight. And as Christian women, we're called not only to pursue social niceties but to serve the lonely and broken of this world as well as build up believers to work for the kingdom.

When we feel overwhelmed by these demands, it's good to take a look at the hospitality shown by Publius, a chief official on the island where the apostle Paul was shipwrecked: "[Publius] welcomed us courteously and fed us for three days. We were showered with honors, and when the time came to sail, people put on board all sorts of things we would need for the trip" (Acts 28:7, 10).

Publius couldn't help but notice the disheveled band of sailors and prisoners that showed up at his door. But the shipwrecked ones near us may not be so obvious. However, if our eyes are open, we'll notice them. Is there a single parent close by who needs a touch of relief and encouragement? How about an elderly neighbor who's fearful and lonely or a disabled and isolated person desperate for contact with a friendly face?

> *It's OK for your house and preparations to be less than perfect—as long as your guests know they're welcome and loved.*
> DEBBIE L. BARKER

It may not be only the lost and unbelieving who need a safe harbor. According to 3 John 1:5, 7-8, we're to "take care of the traveling teachers [fellow Christians] who are passing through," those who "are traveling for the Lord. . . . We ourselves should support them so that we may become partners with them for the truth." Christians get worn out, too, and need an oasis where they can be loved, restored, fed, and prayed for.

No matter the season of life or the limitations of schedule, we can ask the Lord for a heart that's open and the eyes to see those who crave a resting place.

*Lauretta Patterson*

# A Step Further

## Easy Hospitality

1. *Keep it simple*. Sometimes we think of entertaining as creating a sparkling agenda for our guests. But more important is sharing both the joys and heartaches of life. Make your guests part of the family, and they will truly feel at home.

2. *Think seasonally*. If you have three small children at home, your focus should be on making your home open and inviting to them. There will come another season in your life when you'll be able to reach out to others.

3. *Work together*. The body of Christ is meant to function as a healthy unit, taking into account the seasons, gifts, and limitations of each member. Pooling our resources with other members of the body means we can be hospitable far beyond our own abilities.           LP

## Faith Focus

Do you see hospitality as a joy or as something you *have* to do? What steps can you make to fulfill Paul's command in Galatians to serve others "whenever we have the opportunity"?

### Prayer Pointer

Ask God to give you a love for the hurting and a compassion for those who are lost without him. Thank him that he is always hospitable to you. Ask him to reveal to you ways in which you can serve others in your particular season of life.

YOU WILL KEEP IN PERFECT PEACE
ALL WHO TRUST IN YOU, WHOSE
THOUGHTS ARE FIXED ON YOU!
TRUST IN THE LORD ALWAYS, FOR
THE LORD GOD IS THE ETERNAL
ROCK. LORD, WE LOVE TO OBEY
YOUR LAWS; OUR HEART'S DESIRE
IS TO GLORIFY YOUR NAME. ALL
NIGHT LONG I SEARCH FOR YOU;
EARNESTLY I SEEK FOR GOD.

ISAIAH 26:3-4, 8-9

*H*ow do you spend your free time? Do you refinish a favorite chair? Volunteer at a soup kitchen? Listen to music or read a good book? Or do you watch television more than you'd like (either because you need a "brain break" or because you don't have anything else to do)?

If you're hooked on television, you're not alone. But Isaiah tells us to fix our thoughts on God, to earnestly seek him—instead of spending our precious free time on things that won't matter eternally. If you want to kick the too-much-TV habit, here's how.

# Confessions of a TV Addict

When my daughter, Joanna, was born, I planned to carry her with me in a Snugli while I continued my graduate degree. But it took only a few weeks of motherhood (and a lot of screaming!) for me to realize that my tiny daughter wasn't ready for graduate school.

I put my degree on hold and concentrated on keeping Joanna content. Before long, I discovered the one place where she never cried—the rocking chair. Whiling away peaceful hours in a rocking chair may sound idyllic to some, but to me it was like living on a deserted island.

I tried reading to pass the time, but reading while rocking made me seasick. Then, one day, I switched on the TV just as a talk show was getting into full swing. "Our guest today has 101 personalities," said the host, pointing to an ordinary-looking woman seated next to him.

It was downhill from there. For the next four months, while Joanna rocked and nursed blissfully, I plunged deep into the world of daytime TV. Before long, television occupied not only most of my time but most of my thoughts.

One day, a momentous event occurred. Our lease ran out, and we moved to a different apartment. The afternoon we moved in, I switched on the TV only to be greeted by gray fuzz on every channel.

I asked the landlord if we could have an antenna and got a firm "No." It was cable or nothing. I looked imploringly at my husband, who looked regretfully at the checkbook. We just couldn't afford cable service. My world crashed into ruins.

The first two weeks were the hardest. The hours passed

like days. I craved adult companionship and conversation—even if it came only in a "box." Without TV, I felt alone. I tried exercising, which lasted only a week, and baking, which became an excuse to overeat.

I began to spend hours on the phone each week with Denise, a Christian neighbor I'd met at Lamaze class. While Denise sensed God moving in the smallest events of her day, I wondered if he was even there. My cynicism gradually turned into curiosity. Could God be speaking to me? Was he trying to tell me something—only I wasn't listening?

> *As the years have passed, I'm totally convinced the most valuable pursuit I embarked on was that of knowing God.*
>
> KAY ARTHUR

Pregnancy, motherhood, TV—all had provided great distractions from my spiritual doubts. Now, without TV filling my time, I realized just how far I'd moved from God.

As I listened for God's leading, I felt the conviction to read my Bible and pray. The words of Scripture began to soothe my spiritual worries and remind me how deeply my Father loves me.

It's been a year and a half since we moved, and I now care for another child full-time in her home, taking Joanna along with me. There's a big-screen television in the living room, but with the exception of a few well-chosen kids' videos, I almost never watch it. Letting go of television is one of the best things that ever happened to me—because I grew closer to God.          *Betty Smartt Carter*

# A STEP FURTHER

## Turning Off and Tuning In

1. *Tune out.* Start with just one week without television. A mere seven days sounds doable, doesn't it? You might be amazed at how easily you can live without it.
2. *Calculate your savings.* If you currently pay for cable, figure out how much money you'd save for an entire year without it. Or, better yet, figure out how many more hours you'd have in your day if you didn't give in to your couch-potato tendencies.
3. *Make a list.* Write out all the things you could do with those extra hours in your day—go for a walk, listen to classical music, sing hymns, talk with your spouse, chat over coffee with a neighbor, play board games with your kids. Now go out and do them! BSC

## Faith Focus

Think carefully over the past week. How much time did you spend in front of the television? Are you hooked on TV—or could you give it up? How about trying one of the ways to "Turn Off That TV Addiction" this week?

### Prayer Pointer

Ask God to search your heart for anything in your habits that isn't pleasing to him. Then pray for the courage to change those habits, one at a time. Thank him for caring so deeply about you that he wants you to grow closer to him.

WHETHER WE ARE HIGH ABOVE
THE SKY OR IN THE DEEPEST
OCEAN, NOTHING IN ALL CREA-
TION WILL EVER BE ABLE TO SEPA-
RATE US FROM THE LOVE OF GOD
THAT IS REVEALED IN CHRIST JE-
SUS OUR LORD.

ROMANS 8:39

*M*aybe you've just switched occupations—and you're not sure of your skills. Or you recently moved into a different neighborhood, city, or state. Maybe you changed churches, and you don't know where (or even if you have the energy) to start making new friends. Or because of a financial crunch or divorce, you've had to transition from being a stay-at-home mom to working outside the home, and your head is whirling.

We all feel uprooted at times—particularly in this fast-moving society. When you're faced with a move, here's how you can blossom in a new environment.

# It's Moving Time

"I *never* want to move again—ever! I hate this place," I told my mom the first week we'd moved to Montana from Colorado. I was in third grade, and I felt like we had moved to the end of the world. In Colorado we'd spent weekends in the mountains; Montana's flat land stretched barren and treeless for miles. In Colorado, I'd had a best friend, Jorja; in Montana, few "outsiders" moved into our small town, so everyone looked at me as if I had two heads and steered clear.

I was lonely. More than anything I wanted things to go back to the way they were.

If you've ever felt that way about a move—whether it's to another locale, job, or church—you're not alone. A recent survey done by *American Demographics* showed that over 70 percent of Americans move every two or three years—and are unprepared for the emotional challenges of such a transition.

As a child, I was fortunate to have the wisdom of my parents, who had moved many times even before I was born. I remember them saying, "No place on earth will last forever because our real home is with God in heaven. But you can choose whether to be happy—or miserable. And if you want friends, don't wait for other kids to come to you. Go to them."

With each move in my adult life, I've carried those same principles with me.

When my husband, Jeff, and I got married, we lived in a dingy apartment in a not-so-good locale. As a person drawn to things of beauty, I could have been miserable with its odd color combinations and stained carpeting. But instead I sewed bright curtains and pillows for our garage-sale furniture to sidetrack our eyes from the ragged carpeting. And we invited our church's single adults over every Sunday for dinner.

When we moved from a small church to a larger church, we felt the loss of familiar faces each week. So we chose to greet others around us. Soon we had a Bible study going, and the people in that small group became some of our dearest friends.

> *Although our location may change, many things don't: our memories and traditions, the love of close friends and family, and God—who's with us always.*
>
> RAMONA CRAMER TUCKER

But the scariest move I've made was in switching jobs. *I'm successful in my current field,* I told myself when I was in my thirties, *so why should I risk failure?* So I said no to a new job proposal for two years. But God was persistent in his call to a new ministry. In another year, I was ready to risk that transition—and it's been a wonderful, stretching experience.

So, you see, things never did go back to the way they were when I was a third-grader and I'd already lived in New York and Colorado. After Montana, we lived in Saskatchewan, Canada, and then Illinois. And through those moves, I've learned valuable lessons: how to reach out to others, share my faith in varying cultures, treasure my family, and most of all, lean on God, my ultimate "home"!

*Ramona Cramer Tucker*

# A Step Further

## Establishing Roots

1. *Be friendly.* Bake cookies for your new neighbors, coworkers, or church members. Plan a coffee break or a dessert night.
2. *Get involved.* Do what you're passionate about—a moms' group, work Bible study, community outreach—and you'll find others who are passionate about the same things. That's how friendships develop.
3. *Maintain contact with the "special" people from your past to take the edge of loneliness off your move.* But make sure you still have time and energy left to anticipate what God will do in the present and future.
4. *Be patient.* No transition happens overnight. And because it's easy to miss the small joys of life, jot down the good things that happen as a result of your move.
5. *Pray for discernment.* Ask those you trust to pray with you and for you.          RCT

## Faith Focus

At what times in your life have you moved—geograph-
ically, occupationally, or relationally? How have you felt
about those moves? The next time you make a move,
what will you do to smooth the transition for yourself,
your friends, and your family members?

### Prayer Pointer

Ask God to help you deal graciously with the moves of your
life. Tell him specifically the areas
of your life in which you fear
change. Thank him that, no matter where you go, he is always
there to lovingly listen and help.

We will hold to the truth in love, becoming more and more in every way like Christ, who is the head of his body, the church. Under his direction, the whole body is fitted together perfectly. As each part does its own special work, it helps the other parts grow, so that the whole body is healthy and growing and full of love.

EPHESIANS 4:15-16

- "I told him what I thought of him!"
- "She didn't get it, so I had to be honest."
- "I'm only telling you this to help you."

Most of us are taught from childhood on to be honest. But sometimes, especially in this tell-all tabloid culture, we adults can be *too* honest.

In Ephesians 4, the apostle Paul (known for being an outspoken individual) balances honesty—telling others the truth—with love. So before you plunge in and "tell it like it is," here are some words of caution.

# How Honest Is Too Honest?

Most of us crave relationships where communication is open, where we feel free to share our worries, failures, joys, successes, and dreams without fear of censure. We long for people to accept us even when they know about our weaknesses. We want friends who will love us anyway.

But can we be too open? too transparent? Is there a point where honesty ends and hurt begins?

To be *transparent* is to be "without guile or concealment; open; frank; candid." To many, that means being able to say without restraint whatever pops into your mind. This "no-holds-barred" approach fosters intimacy, we are told, so we yield to its appeal until we discover that it can destroy the very relationships we hold dear.

Why is transparency destructive at times? To begin with, feelings and thoughts are extremely changeable. My reactions may vary from month to month—even hour to hour. I'm hard put at times to know which is the real me. To allow a loved one to be the dumping ground for temporary feelings is not only inconsiderate but also possibly dishonest.

And transparency often isn't kind. Cleaning the barbecue grill has got to head the list of the Ten Most Revolting Jobs around my house. But one hot August afternoon, I decided that before we had company over for hamburgers the next day, the grill had to be cleaned. Perspiring profusely, I scrubbed away.

In the middle of the job, I hastened into the kitchen for more paper towels. Jack, who was trying hard to exercise regularly, was resting with his feet up on an ottoman. "I walked five miles today," he said proudly.

Between clenched teeth, I replied, "Boy, think what you could have accomplished with all that energy!"

I watched the joy of accomplishment drain from Jack's face like water from an unplugged sink. I immediately wanted to reach into the air and pull back my words.

I'd been transparent, all right—I'd said exactly what I'd been thinking at that moment. But I was totally wrong in saying it because it was unkind.

*Do you take kindness on and off, depending on your mood or whom you're with? Often, we save our kind behavior for people we seldom see, and we're least kind to the people we're with every day.*
MARY WHELCHEL

Proverbs 3:3 tells me, "Never let loyalty and kindness get away from you! Wear them like a necklace; write them deep within your heart." If what we call *transparency* is really *bluntness,* if it is unkind and unloving, then we are disobeying this command and honesty is not the best policy. According to Scripture, truth must be married to love; honesty must be intertwined with kindness.

As we seek to build depth and intimacy in communication, we need wisdom and discretion. Proverbs 2:11 says, "Wise planning will watch over you. Understanding will keep you safe."

As we seek the guidance of the Holy Spirit, we will understand what biblical honesty really is. It is not transparency, as some would have us believe, but true words spoken in love and kindness to build up, not tear down, those we value.

*Carole Mayhall*

# A Step Further

### Honesty—the Best Policy?

1. *Lighten up.* Real love overlooks idiosyncrasies, faults, inconsistencies, and irritations. Would you want others sharing what they think all the time— even when the meal you've just slaved over for dinner tastes like sawdust? Give others the same slack you'd like to receive.

2. *Check your motivation.* Is it constructive criticism or just criticism you're about to dish out? Search your heart, and pray for wisdom.

3. *Use discretion.* Know when to speak and when to keep silent. Wisdom, under-standing, and discretion come only from knowing ever more deeply the one who personifies wisdom—Jesus Christ.    CM

## Faith Focus

How honest are you—too honest? not honest enough?
In what situations has honesty *not* been the best policy
with your family, friends, or fellow church members?
What will you think about the next time you're tempted
to "tell it like it is"?

*Prayer Pointer*

Thank God for granting you wisdom and understanding when you ask for them. Pray that the Holy Spirit will put a seal on your lips so that you will speak the truth only in love and won't use honesty to hurt others.

THERE MUST BE A SPIRITUAL RE-
NEWAL OF YOUR THOUGHTS AND
ATTITUDES. YOU MUST DISPLAY A
NEW NATURE BECAUSE YOU ARE A
NEW PERSON, CREATED IN GOD'S
LIKENESS—RIGHTEOUS, HOLY, AND
TRUE.

EPHESIANS 4:23-24

*D*o you ever wish you had your friend's house? That you didn't have to get by with your old couch for one more year? That you could take off on a cruise to the Bahamas like your wealthy neighbors? That you didn't receive any advertisements so you wouldn't have to hear your kids whine, "Gimme that toy. Please, Mom?" or "I want that candy!"

Ephesians 4:23-24 offers an antidote to the ever-growing wishes and wants of our materialistic world. It calls us to renewed thoughts and attitudes. If you crave a cure for the "gimmes," read on.

# Do You Have the "Gimmes"?

Leaving our seven-year-old "handyman special" home, my husband, Kurt, and I hopped in the car and drove to visit relatives in their new, custom-built, no-less-than-the-best mansion. I breathed a prayer that envy wouldn't get the best of us. But it did.

After a weekend together enjoying all the household amenities money can buy, it was time to leave. Happy for our relatives, and unhappy for us, we left their spacious home and returned to ours, which by that time seemed like an oversized garage.

When we bought a small house in a neighborhood of big, pretentious homes, the real-estate agents failed to tell us that every time we'd take a walk, we'd go for a gawk. King Solomon once said, "A heart at peace gives life to the body, but envy rots the bones" (Prov. 14:30, NIV). How true. Every time we'd envy, we'd feel rotten!

Our battle made me wonder to what extent others were affected by envy. I asked some friends, and their answers held few surprises. Couples without a house envy those who have one. Women battling the bulge envy others with a pencil-thin figure. No one is immune.

Based on research, friendly counsel, and our own experiences, Kurt and I have learned a few precautionary measures that have kept us content with what we have.

After realizing and repenting of our envy problem, we started questioning our values. A survey of twenty-five thousand people conducted by *Psychology Today* magazine showed that people desiring wealth, fame, popularity, and beauty were more apt to envy than those who did not desire those attributes. This should cause us, particularly as Christians, to question our values. Do our treasures lie in the wrong chest? Are we busy chasing after the temporary things of this world rather than the eternal blessings and characteristics of Christ?

Also, putting our envy in perspective helps our family tremendously. We videotaped a World Vision TV fund-raiser for a reminder that we already have more than we need. Our boys didn't believe their eyes when they viewed the wretched conditions on the other side of the world. Gaining a more global perspective made us acutely aware of all we do have instead of all those things we don't.

> *The more time we spend alone with God,*
> *the more his attitudes will rub off on us.*
> JILL BRISCOE

After living ten years in our home, we are now financially at a point where we can afford to move to a bigger, better one. But we've chosen to raise our boys in our less-than-average dwelling. At the same time, we are supporting a few missionaries, who don't even live in a home, and a Third-World child who wouldn't otherwise have money for food or inoculations.

We now renovate our goals, rather than our home. Will our children miss a big family room with a wood-burning fireplace? Like us, they probably will from time to time. But we've learned we don't need a fireplace to have a fireside chat.                    *Paige Jaeger*

# A STEP FURTHER

## Beating the Green-Eyed Monster

1. *Admit your envy.* Recognize and admit to yourself and to God that envy exists. Pinpointing the object of your envy helps you focus your energy as you begin correcting the problem.
2. *Thank God for the "little" things.* It's easy to be thankful for big surprises and abundant blessings, but we often fail to be grateful for our everyday provisions.
3. *Filter out "gimme" propaganda.* Successful advertising aims at increasing dissatisfaction and/or creating a need we didn't know we had. Reject this so-called need before Madison Avenue convinces you otherwise.
4. *Anticipate envy.* If you know what situations or people trigger envious feelings in you, pray in advance for the strength to resist this temptation. PJ

## Faith Focus

Do you struggle with envy? If so, in what areas? What steps do you need to take to beat the green-eyed monster of envy and be satisfied with what you have?

### *Prayer Pointer*

Thank God for being all-sufficient, for always supplying your needs (many times even before you pray for them). Ask him to take envy out of your life and to help you focus on his abundant provisions instead.

The Lord is good and does what is right; he shows the proper path to those who go astray. He leads the humble in what is right, teaching them his way. The Lord leads with unfailing love and faithfulness all those who keep his covenant and obey his decrees.

Psalm 25:8-10

*I*f a friend was asked to describe you, what would she say? Recently I asked one of my good friends—eighteen years running—to describe me. Laughingly she said, "That's easy. You're a chatterbox, you never sit still, and you're always up to something!"

I guess it's obvious I'm one of those people who prefer life "on the move." But my busy spirit can be both good (I get a lot of things done) and hard (when quieter-spirited folks feel I'm not listening to them as I buzz around).

If you're striving for that humble balance (Ps. 25), this next devotional will help.

# Confessions of a Woman on the Whirl

My husband, Jim, says I have chronic PMS—"Perpetual Martha Syndrome." He'll attest that, like Martha of Bethany—who welcomed Jesus into her home for dinner but didn't have time to sit and listen to him—I have a tough time sitting still. It's just that there's so much to do and the list is never ending!

I've heard countless sermons on the story of Martha's dinner party (Luke 10:38-42), and basically, they've all criticized Martha, the one busily preparing a meal for all her guests, and glorified Mary, the one quietly sitting at Christ's feet.

Inevitably, my response to such sermons has been a great wave of guilt and conviction, followed by a note to myself on the fridge in big, bold letters: "BE MARY . . . NOT MARTHA!"

For the next week or two I'd try to be Mary; I'd try to sit quietly and listen to the Lord. But soon I'd be picking lint fuzz balls from the couch as my mind raced ahead to my to-do list. I'd catch myself making mental memos of calls to make while bathing the dog, then making those calls on the cordless phone while pruning the roses. Might as well wave bye-bye to Mary. Martha was back!

One afternoon, while I was praying as I scrubbed the kitchen floor, it hit me—maybe Martha wasn't such a misdirected gal after all. Maybe all she needed was a microwave! Sure, she didn't have her priorities in order—but hey, if it weren't for Martha, no one would've eaten! Could it be that the Martha in me was a gift, provided I used it for good and not guilt?

Soon after, Martha's story came up at my Bible study. My

teacher, Kris, said, "Wouldn't you love going to her house for dinner? She'd make everything lovely and delicious . . . the original Martha Stewart!"

We made a list of Martha's personality traits. In her favor, she had the gift of hospitality. She opened her heart and her home to Jesus. She had a servant's heart and a teachable spirit. When Jesus corrected her, she received his criticism. She was a woman of action whose biggest shortcoming was her self-righteous complaining about her sister, Mary.

> *During our seasons of busyness, we must stop to ask: Does what we're doing have a greater claim on our allegiance than spending time with our Lord?*
>
> KAREN HEFFNER

Jesus never told Martha to be Mary; he told her not to worry about unimportant things. Jesus didn't order Mary to help Martha, but he didn't order Martha to stop serving and sit at his feet either. Preparing the meal was a valuable service, but Martha's grumbling detracted from her good deed. Martha wasn't so bad—she just needed an attitude adjustment!

I realize I'll always be a Martha. After wrestling with her for almost a decade, I've learned, as Popeye said, "I yam what I yam." But rather than striving to be Mary, I can strive to be the best of Martha—the transformed Martha with the servant's heart and the teachable spirit. I know now that the Lord has given me certain strengths and weaknesses—and depending on how I handle it, my busyness can be either.

*Suzanne M. Grissom*

# A Step Further

## Making the Most of Martha

1. *Question your motives.* Are you serving yourself or the Lord? Are you going on your own strength or his? Are you driven or called—and who's in the driver's seat?
2. *Master moderation.* Instead of being the director of your local crisis pregnancy center, why not just help as a hotline counselor? Your ministries—and other activities—don't have to be all or nothing.
3. *Learn how to say no.* You may have to practice this a few times, but if your schedule's full, God doesn't give a green light. Or if your family hasn't had a home-cooked meal in two weeks, just say no.
4. *Make people a priority.* Remember that the point of having guests over is not to win the clean-kitchen award but to enjoy their company.                    SMG

## Faith Focus

Are you a woman on the whirl—or do you wish you were busier? Are you struggling to balance the many important facets of your life and you don't know how to get it all done? If you tend to be a Martha, which tips above would help you make the most of the personality and gifts God has given you?

### Prayer Pointer

Thank God for his wonderful act of creating you. Ask him to lead you toward the activities you should be doing and to help you say no to those he's not calling you to do. Pray for wisdom in balancing the various aspects of your life and commitments.

MAY YOUR ROOTS GO DOWN DEEP
INTO THE SOIL OF GOD'S MARVEL-
OUS LOVE. AND MAY YOU HAVE
THE POWER TO UNDERSTAND, AS
ALL GOD'S PEOPLE SHOULD, HOW
WIDE, HOW LONG, HOW HIGH,
AND HOW DEEP HIS LOVE REALLY
IS. MAY YOU EXPERIENCE THE
LOVE OF CHRIST, THOUGH IT IS SO
GREAT YOU WILL NEVER FULLY
UNDERSTAND IT.

EPHESIANS 3:17-19

*L*ove and romance—who doesn't long for them? Whether we find them in romance novels, movies, soap operas, or those "special moments" of a dating relationship or marriage, it's important to feel loved and wanted. Even the Bible includes tender and sizzling scenes and descriptions of romantic love (see Song of Songs).

But when romantic love becomes the thing we crave, Scripture tells us we've missed the boat. There's only one love that is wide enough and deep enough to satisfy: God's love (Eph. 3).

Who or what is satisfying your deepest needs? Maybe it's time to take a look.

# Hooked on Romance

When my husband, Rick, and I moved to Southern California in 1977, my life seemed far from under my control. Neither of us had wanted to make the move, but that's where his job took us.

I had my three children in quick succession. Since I didn't know anybody, I built my life around them—and around reading. Romance novels camouflaged how I really felt— isolated and miserable.

I began voraciously devouring westerns, sensual historical novels, gothic romances, and realized, *I can write this.* Eventually I published thirteen novels in the mainstream market—and they met with success, selling roughly three million copies.

Writing became increasingly important to me; it was my escape. I could control the characters in my books when I couldn't control the people in my life. Rick worked long hours—leaving early in the morning, coming home late, exhausted, with little energy left for me and our children—so I began pumping a lot of energy into creating my stories.

But my passion for romance novels was taking its toll. At one point, Rick told me, "If you had a choice between your writing and the kids and me, you'd take your writing." It was a shock—but he was right.

We decided we needed to make some changes. We moved again, this time back to northern California, where Rick started his own business. Despite all the external changes, inside we were spiritually starving, though we didn't know it at the time. We were fighting a lot.

Out of curiosity, I accepted a neighbor's invitation to

church a few weeks after our move. The warmth and love I felt in that congregation drew me back again and again. I started taking my kids with me, then Rick came along. Our lives began to change—not from the outside, but from the inside out. When Christ became our personal Savior, Rick and I were baptized together. Our children soon followed.

*The priority you place on time with God affects your intimacy. Women who invest more time in their spiritual life are significantly more likely to say they're satisfied and have fewer drought times.*
CAROLE MAYHALL AND LYNN MAYHALL WESTBERG

Since I've become a Christian, I've learned I need to choose things that enlighten, encourage, and assist me in my walk with Christ. Sometimes I'll feel uncomfortable when I'm reading a book or watching a movie, and I'll have to toss the book out or change the channel. I allow God to soften my heart to the point where I'm sensitive to what the Holy Spirit tells me. Obedience is my loving response to my heavenly Father (which is why I didn't write again until I'd spent several years studying God's Word).

Now I'm writing Christian romance novels instead; several of my characters have been inspired by people and events in the Bible. I've learned that the entire Bible is a love story—filled with God's love for us. The media tells us romance and sex are what count, not relationship. But what we really need is Jesus' love and a relationship with him. Only then can our deepest needs be satisfied—something no novel can ever do.                *Francine Rivers*

# A Step Further

## Breaking Free

1. *Get to the heart of the problem.* If you find yourself steeped in reading or watching romance, ask yourself, *What's missing in my life? Am I hiding from emotional pain or loneliness?* Seek to solve the real problem instead of escaping it.

2. *Redefine love.* Many romance novels' definition of *love* is shallow—a man and woman can fulfill all their needs (including sexual desires before marriage) between themselves without God. Read 1 Corinthians 13 for a refresher course in *real* love.

3. *Go to the source of romance.* The desire for romance isn't wrong; it's God-given. God made sexual desire to be a blessing—in the context of marriage. Ask the Author of romance to help you meet these desires in healthy ways.     FR

## Faith Focus

How much time do you spend searching for romance in your life (i.e., reading romance novels, watching soap operas, expecting gestures from your husband or boyfriend)? Why? If you're hooked on romance, what one step can you take today to redirect your passion toward a relationship with God?

### Prayer Pointer

Thank God for being the Creator of love and for loving you. Ask him to help you enjoy the moments of romance in your life without making them a priority. Pray for discernment—that your thought energy and time will be used wisely and eternally for his kingdom.

WE ALL MAKE MANY MISTAKES, BUT THOSE WHO CONTROL THEIR TONGUES CAN ALSO CONTROL THEMSELVES IN EVERY OTHER WAY. WE CAN MAKE A LARGE HORSE TURN AROUND AND GO WHEREVER WE WANT BY MEANS OF A SMALL BIT IN ITS MOUTH. AND A TINY RUDDER MAKES A HUGE SHIP TURN WHEREVER THE PILOT WANTS IT TO GO, EVEN THOUGH THE WINDS ARE STRONG.

JAMES 3:2-4

*D*o you ever think:

- *Why did I say that? I'll never be able to take it back.*
- *Why is it so easy for me to yell at my family?*
- *Why did I make that phone call when I was mad?*

When I was young, children often taunted each other on the playground with: "Sticks and stones may break my bones, but words will never hurt me." But guess what—they were wrong. Words can hurt—and as growing Christians, God calls us to control our tongues (James 3).

# Taming the Tongue

I had just finished sharing my personal testimony with a large group of businesswomen and was in the restroom repairing my makeup when a woman walked in.

"Do you remember me?" she asked. I glanced at her name tag, but neither her face nor her name was familiar.

"I'm sorry," I apologized, but she cut me off abruptly.

"Five years ago, you wrote me a very mean letter. It hurt me deeply, and I've saved it all these years, hoping someday I'd run into you again."

My face blushed crimson as I struggled between humiliation and confusion. I had no idea what this woman was referring to, and my mind was racing too fast to think clearly.

"I owned an antique shop," she continued, "and after shopping in my store, you wrote a letter complaining about my rudeness."

Reeling from her accusation, I could think of only one thing to do. I grabbed her hand and said, "I'm very sorry to have hurt you. Please forgive me." The woman pulled back her hand, nodded slightly, then stalked out.

I fled to my car, barely making it before bursting into tears. To think my words had so devastated someone she had harbored them for five years, and I couldn't even remember the incident! What a hypocrite I must have sounded like as she'd listened to my speech! I leaned my head against the steering wheel and sobbed, "God, forgive me for my careless words."

Later that evening, as I looked back through my journals, I discovered an entry about the occurrence. The woman had loudly criticized a friend with whom I was shopping for handling a vase. She had embarrassed us, making us feel like sticky-fingered children. I had thought a letter was more than justified—she deserved it! But now my motive seemed impulsive and self-centered. I really had wanted to make her feel as bad as she'd made me feel.

Soon after, I read in my Bible about the woman who was caught in adultery. The Pharisees were correct, though merciless, in their accusations. But when they dragged her before Christ, he rebuked the Pharisees, not the woman.

> *It's important to remember that our words reflect the state of our heart towards God.*
> JAN DARGATZ

After the Pharisees left Christ alone with her, he asked where her accusers were and whether any of them condemned her.

"No one, sir," she said.

"Then neither do I condemn you," Jesus declared. "Go now and leave your life of sin" (John 8:11, NIV).

The difference between our two confrontations was glaring! Jesus had confronted this woman in a way that kept her open to him. I'd confronted the store owner in a way that built walls of resentment.

I've longed for another chance with the woman in the restroom. I've mentally rewritten that letter a thousand times and see many kinder ways I could have said the same thing. But in the process, I've learned a tremendous lesson. Words are too valuable to toss around without a thought. Used carelessly, they alienate. But when used carefully, words can build bridges—to Christ.               *Mayo Mathers*

# A Step Further

## Managing Your Mouth

1. *Remember the adage Count to ten.* It works wonders in calming down your spirit before you open your mouth.
2. *Steep yourself in Scripture.* Books such as James and Proverbs are great antidotes to opening your mouth too hastily.
3. *Put yourself in the other person's shoes.* When you do this, anger and irritation often dissipate.
4. *Be gracious.* Scripture tells us that a soft answer turns away wrath, so give others grace—as God gives you grace, even when you don't deserve it.
5. *Decide how you want your words to be used.* Do you want them to further your own causes, vindicate yourself, or make yourself feel better? Or do you want them to point the way to Christ?  RCT

## Faith Focus

How careful are you with your words? Do you tend to
spout words when you're angry—or do you just stay
quiet and think nasty thoughts? The next time you're
tempted to let someone have it (and maybe deservedly
so), what will you choose to say?

*Prayer Pointer*

Thank God for his patience with
you. Praise him for being a merci-
ful, gracious, compassionate
God. Ask him to help you pass on
that mercy, grace, and compassion to others in the words you
choose to use (and not use).

FAN INTO FLAMES THE SPIRITUAL
GIFT GOD GAVE YOU WHEN I LAID
MY HANDS ON YOU. FOR GOD HAS
NOT GIVEN US A SPIRIT OF FEAR
AND TIMIDITY, BUT OF POWER,
LOVE, AND SELF-DISCIPLINE.

2 TIMOTHY 1:6-7

$\mathcal{W}$hat comes to your mind when you hear the word *shy*? A three-year-old who clings to her mother's skirts? A college freshman who's afraid to ask anyone for directions to her class? The single parent in your church who sits alone, fearful she won't be accepted?

Those who are shy know that even daily life can be painful. But God promises not to leave us alone; he gives us "power, love, and self-discipline." If you struggle with shyness, here's how to make the best of your bashfulness.

# Are You Shy like Me?

Walking into the grocery store one afternoon, I noticed Judy's car in the parking lot. Once inside, I peeked around the corner of each aisle to make sure she couldn't catch me unaware. When I saw her leave, I was relieved I wouldn't have to talk to her. After all, making conversation with others was agony for me.

Shy women endure embarrassments like this daily. We talk to our children's teachers, and our hands shake. Our neighbor's dog takes over our yard, and we fume—to ourselves.

We can fool ourselves into thinking that shyness isn't so bad, yet it encourages a self-conscious preoccupation—a fixation that fosters depression, anxiety, and loneliness. And these attitudes erect substantial roadblocks to growing in God's love.

I knew God couldn't be pleased with my sneaking around in grocery stores to avoid talking to other people. I also longed for the spirit of power, love, and self-discipline Paul talked about in 2 Timothy. I knew that in order to show God's love to others, my shyness had to go.

So I began doing research. I evaluated which situations or types of people made me shy and discovered that certain categories of people intimidate me. Now when I know I'll be around such persons, I think of conversational topics ahead of time.

I also realized shyness is often related to low self-esteem. We think we have nothing important to contribute compared to everyone else, who seems so talented and capable. Instead of nursing the foggy notion that I was awkward and unattractive, I identified specific personal pluses and minuses. Sure, my figure was not picture-perfect, but my complexion glowed. I accentuated my face with better skin care and makeup and toned my shape with exercise.

I also learned we can build our self-esteem by finding what we do well and then doing it. When my friend Barb taught English to refugees, she tried so hard to communicate that her self-consciousness faded. That success helped her relate better to others.

Social prowess also grows as we care about others. People were drawn to Jesus not only because of his remarkable power and authority but also because he was interested in them.

> *I don't need to be intimidated by the gifts God's given other people. I just need to be faithful to use the ones he's given me.*
> RAMONA CRAMER TUCKER

One night as I sat silently at a party, I felt sorry for the woman next to me who was quiet, too. So I opened up to try to make her feel better. I felt so good about helping her that I later tried to draw others out, seeing myself as the "shy person's rescue squad."

For Christian women, stepping out of shyness can be a spiritual journey. God stretches our faith as we rely on his love and claim his promise, "Love has no fear because perfect love expels all fear" (1 John 4:18). As we overcome shyness, we gain confidence to tackle other problems in life.

And if you're like me, it makes it easier to go grocery shopping, too.                    *Jan Johnson*

# A Step Further

## Confidence Boosters

1. *Find the source.* Identify what situations make you feel shy.
2. *Ask questions.* Develop a list of ritual questions about jobs, family members, and hobbies to use in social situations.
3. *Practice.* Strike up conversations while standing in line at banks, grocery stores, and amusement parks to increase both your experience and confidence.
4. *Use the "soften" touch.* Arthur Wassmer, in his book *Making Contact* (Dial Press), suggests that shy people use the positive nonverbal signals of the acronym *soften:* smile, open posture, forward lean, touch, eye contact, nod.
5. *Start a warm-fuzzy file.* For a confidence boost, keep a file of awards, thank-you notes, and letters of appreciation to remind you that God is able to use you.

JJ

**Faith Focus**

On a scale of one (shy) to ten (bold), where would you rate your personality? How do you look at shyness—as something that holds a person back or as an opportunity to be sensitive to others? If you're shy, how will you step out and take a risk this week? If you're bold, what's one way you can be sensitive to a shy friend, coworker, or family member?

*Prayer Pointer*

Praise God for knowing you intimately. Thank him for the personality he's given you—even the characteristics you don't like. Then ask him to help you bring honor to his name as you learn to use the uniqueness of your personality to reach out to others.

You are citizens along with all of God's holy people. You are members of God's family. We are his house, built on the foundation of the apostles and the prophets. And the cornerstone is Christ Jesus himself. We who believe are carefully joined together, becoming a holy temple for the Lord.

EPHESIANS 2:19-21

*I*f someone asked you who you are, what would you say? Maybe you'd say that you're a stay-at-home mom, a wife, a career woman, a Sunday school teacher, a single parent. But what happens when those labels are removed? We may feel lost, as if we don't really know who we are.

Although labels may be true, they're not what God sees when he looks at you. According to Ephesians, he sees you as his child, part of the family of God.

So if you can't answer the question, "Who are you?" without giving yourself a label, maybe it's time for a deeper look.

# Who Am I *Really?*

I went through a difficult time shortly after my daughter was born. Wanting to spend as much time with her as possible, I decided to work at home rather than immediately return to the workplace. But I quickly discovered I'd underestimated how much having a title, office, and regular paycheck contributed to my sense of self. I was thrilled to be a mother—but I mourned the loss of my identity as a briefcase-carrying career woman.

My friend Barbara went through the opposite experience. She'd spent most of her adult life happily raising four children. When her youngest son went off to college, Barbara found herself adrift. "I felt I had no purpose in life anymore," she recalls. She briefly took a job as a receptionist at a bank but found her new role as a working woman an unsatisfying substitute for the one she missed so desperately.

The phrase *identity crisis* has become something of a cliché. But the problem behind the phrase is painfully real. In our rapidly changing society, where roles and relationships—the things we typically base our identity on—are in constant flux, an identity crisis is all too common.

Barbara and I made the same mistake—we based our identities on external life circumstances that are subject to change. But recognizing the problem is easier than finding a solution.

Through firsthand experience, I discovered that the first step in developing a true identity is to be rooted in Christ. "Human relationships always fall short," says psychologist Beverly Grall. "But when you have a strong faith in Jesus Christ—and a strong sense of who you are in that relationship with him—you've uncovered the most dependable foundation there is for building an accurate sense of your identity."

I found it's also important to know yourself, not just your roles. For example, if I define myself simply as a mother, I will be devastated when my children grow up and my mothering role diminishes. But if I define myself as someone with a talent for nurturing, I'll retain my identity and find other ways to express it—even when confronted with an empty nest.

Questioning who we are is never easy, but it can serve a useful purpose—if we let it. "Pain gets our attention," says Grall. "We often grow much closer to God when we've experienced brokenness. In the same way, we often become better acquainted with ourselves when we go through difficult experiences as well."

> *The more time I spend with God, the more confident I am in him—and in myself.*
> CYNTHIA CLAWSON

I can attest to that. I probably never would have been sufficiently motivated to seriously inventory my gifts—and consequently develop who I am in Christ as my foundation—had I not experienced the pain and emptiness of losing my old identity.

But now, as a result of God's work and some of my own, I feel much more confident in who I am in Christ—in whatever circumstances I find myself in in life. And that's a liberating feeling. *Janis Long Harris*

# A Step Further

## Discovering Your *Real* Identity

1. *Make God your anchor.* Establish a strong spiritual identity rooted in a relationship with God—the only truly reliable relationship that exists.

2. *Discover your spiritual gifts.* When you derive your identity more from the gifts you have rather than from a specific way of exercising them, you won't lose your sense of self when your circumstances change.

3. *Grow through pain.* Emptying yourself of an old identity can be scary, uncertain, and exhausting. But it's important— because it allows God the space he needs to do his work in you.          JLH

## Faith Focus

How would you define yourself? Write down any words you can think of. How can you turn those labels into character qualities? (For example, a Sunday school teacher is someone who loves working with children.) What steps do you need to take today to broaden your horizons beyond the labels you've been giving yourself?

### Prayer Pointer

Thank God that he has called you to be a member of his family. Ask him to give you creativity as you think beyond labels to who you really are: his unique, specially loved child. Then ask him to give you opportunities to use your gifts to nurture others.

GET RID OF ALL BITTERNESS, RAGE, ANGER, HARSH WORDS, AND SLANDER, AS WELL AS ALL TYPES OF MALICIOUS BEHAVIOR. INSTEAD, BE KIND TO EACH OTHER, TENDERHEARTED, FORGIVING ONE ANOTHER, JUST AS GOD THROUGH CHRIST HAS FORGIVEN YOU.

EPHESIANS 4:31-32

*A* friend stands you up for a lunch date. Your spouse walks out on your ten-year marriage. A respected church member falls into sin. Your sister gossips about you. And you wonder, *How can I ever forgive that person for all the hurt?*

But that's exactly what God calls us to do. Ephesians 4 gives us a glimpse of the kind of forgiving heart and spirit God wants us to have—and why.

If you're wrestling with whether or not to forgive a person who's hurt you, read on for what forgiveness is—and what it's not.

# Forgiving Others

We all know we're supposed to forgive one another—but it's a lot easier said than done. And sometimes when we forgive others, we still feel hurt or a relational conflict remains unresolved. Is "I forgive you" just a phrase we utter for the sake of holy appearances, or does it really do some good? What exactly is forgiveness, anyway?

*Forgiveness is a choice, not an emotion.* God knows how unreliable and vacillating our emotions are. A simple shift in hormones or brain chemicals is all it takes for us to feel at odds with life. But when we choose to forgive, God sends grace to do the healing.

*Forgiveness is breaking the power of pain, anger, and hatred.* When a person wrongs me, it's in my power to forgive—whether or not that person ever acknowledges what she did to me, feels sorry about it, or changes her ways. My forgiveness not only expresses the power I have, it also breaks the power the wrongdoer has over me. When I've worked through the hurt and the anger and made the choice to forgive, I'm saying, in essence, I release you from your guilt in relation to me. I will no longer be manipulated by the memory of this.

*Forgiveness is a process.* Wounds take time to heal. The deeper the wound, the longer the recovery. Either a wound heals or it gets infected and spreads poison to other parts of the body. Forgiveness makes it possible for our inner wounds to heal. On an emotional level, you may still feel the hurt, but if you're consistently choosing to forgive, eventually that person, that situation, loses its power over you.

When the apostle Peter asked Jesus how many times he

should forgive a person, Jesus replied, "Seventy times seven" (Matt. 18:22). In other words, don't keep score. Rather than supply a neat formula, easy for a self-righteous person to carry out, our Lord described—and demonstrated—a way of life.

*Forgiveness is an act of grace.* Forgiveness is one act we can perform that mirrors the character of God. When we extend his grace to another human being, we're acting as God's conduit to a wounded world. A friend may, in time, earn back my trust, but she can't earn my forgiveness; I must give it willingly, freely.

> *Before we are able to feel compassion or alleviate discord, we have to recognize God's unconditional forgiveness of our sins and adopt that same attitude.*
> JUDITH LECHMAN

In the last few years, I've become more willing to forgive because I've begun to recognize how much I need forgiveness myself. I understand how easy it is to sin against another person. I get caught up in circumstances and emotions. There may be a logical reason for my behavior—but I've still sinned, and I need to be forgiven. When I view a wrongdoer in this same way, forgiving that person isn't such a huge leap after all.

When we try to get even, the cycle of hurt never ends. But when we forgive, we stop evil cold. We give a sinner like ourselves another chance. And we free ourselves to live and grow in the bountiful grace of God.

*Vinita Hampton Wright*

# A STEP FURTHER

## What Forgiveness Is Not

1. *Forgetting.* If an offense is serious enough to need forgiveness, then it's too serious to wipe from memory. Forgetting offenses such as betrayal or broken vows violates our sense of justice. But our memory of the wrong, when healed by forgiveness, ceases to be obsessive and destructive.

2. *An open door for more wrongdoing.* A woman may forgive her husband for beating her up, but she's under no moral obligation to remain in a position to be abused again. Forgiveness isn't a substitute for discipline in the home or for law enforcement in the community.

3. *Resolution.* True reconciliation requires not only that forgiveness be asked both ways but also that guilt be clarified and agreed upon, and real sorrow expressed.

VHW

## Faith Focus

Is there someone you need to forgive (a family member, church staffer, even yourself)? What step can you take in that direction this week so you can begin the healing process?

### Prayer Pointer

Thank God for being the Great Forgiver—for forgiving your sins through the death of Jesus Christ on the cross. Ask God to help you forgive others as he has forgiven you (even when you think they don't deserve it).

WITHOUT WAVERING, LET US
HOLD TIGHTLY TO THE HOPE WE
SAY WE HAVE, FOR GOD CAN BE
TRUSTED TO KEEP HIS PROMISE.
THINK OF WAYS TO ENCOURAGE
ONE ANOTHER TO OUTBURSTS OF
LOVE AND GOOD DEEDS. AND LET
US NOT NEGLECT OUR MEETING
TOGETHER, AS SOME PEOPLE DO,
BUT ENCOURAGE . . . EACH OTHER.

HEBREWS 10:23-25

DAY 25

$\mathcal{D}$id you know . . . ?" The gossip hotline. We've all been part of it—whether as giver, receiver, or subject. Gossip is powerful. Just one phone call or whispered conversation has the ability to tear apart lives, destroy reputations, end careers, and wreck families.

But gossip doesn't have to be a negative influence. As Hebrews 10:24 says, we can "encourage one another to outbursts of love and good deeds."

So how does this good gossip work? Check out the following ideas from author Dandi Daley Mackall—and then pass them along.

# Good Gossip

When I joined a sorority my first year at college, I felt unsophisticated and a little intimidated by my older sorority sisters. Would I ever fit in? I wondered. Then one night, about a week into my first semester, my roommate in the sorority passed on a conversation she'd had at dinner. "Sue told me she likes to sit by you at meals because you're so witty."

Nothing could have surprised me more! I didn't think Sue even knew who I was, and the last thing I felt was witty. If Sue herself had complimented me on my dinner conversation, I would have assumed she felt sorry for me and was trying to be nice. But since Sue had complimented me to my roommate, I couldn't pass off her comment as flattery. While my roommate was passing on a personal comment someone else had made—she was gossiping—that secondhand information dramatically changed the way I felt about myself! It was good gossip.

Scripture repeatedly reminds us that the tongue wields tremendous power to damage or heal others: "Some people make cutting remarks, but the words of the wise bring healing" (Prov. 12:18); and "the godly give good advice, but fools are destroyed by their lack of common sense" (Prov. 10:21). When we maliciously pass along information to hurt someone else or to gain attention for ourselves, we've sinned. Yet kind, encouraging words carry the same powerful potential to affect others—for good. Each day we make a choice about what information we'll take from conversations and repeat to other people.

Laurie's son, Craig, played junior-high soccer, and she was used to hearing from the coaches or other mothers about how rambunctious Craig was at practice or at games. But when she finally heard a compliment, Laurie wasn't sure what to do with it.

"One of the other mothers who had helped out hauling the boys around came up to me after the last game. 'I just wanted to tell you that your son, Craig, is such a gentleman,' she said. 'Whenever he rode with us, he always thanked us and was respectful.' I was so flabbergasted, I don't even know if I thanked her!"

*People who are good for you will encourage the positive—not the negative—in you.*
Eileen Silva Kindig

Laurie admitted, "Craig hears from me every single time someone reports to me about how bad he is. But I need to go home right now and tell him about this good report!"

Like Laurie, we rarely register these secondhand compliments—or if we do, we fail to pass them on to the people who would benefit most from them. Whether it's sharing at a prayer meeting how an absent believer is walking in faith or telling your daughter that her father mentioned to you how responsible she's becoming, praise is meant to be repeated. So take advantage of the tremendous opportunities to edify and encourage that all too often pass by unnoticed.

Instead of using the power of our tongue for evil, use it for good. Spread kind words—and let good news travel fast! *Dandi Daley Mackall*

# A STEP FURTHER

## Pass On the Praise!

1. *Look for the good in others.* Do you see that woman on your church committee who's always late as irresponsible—or as a good mother who's taking a few extra minutes to check on her kids? If we want to build others up with "good gossip," we first need to catch them being good.

2. *Pass it on.* Once you catch someone being an exceptional friend or student or cook, don't keep it to yourself! Tell others. And when you hear others complimenting a mutual friend or acquaintance, share the kind words.

3. *Give gossip a positive spin.* It may be fun to share gossip, but it takes courage to reverse it. When gossip is passed on to you, find a way to pass along a blessing in its place.                DDM

## Faith Focus

Have you ever been the recipient of gossip? or passed along gossip? Was it for the good—or for the bad? The next time you have the opportunity to pass along gossip, which kind will it be? When someone tries to share with you the bad variety, how will you respond?

*Prayer Pointer*

Ask God to give you a nudge when needed so that the only gossip that crosses your lips is the good variety. Thank him for loving you so much that he's fine-tuning you to be an instrument of his praise—in one area at a time.

Everything else is worthless when compared with the priceless gain of knowing Christ Jesus my Lord. I have discarded everything else, counting it all as garbage, so that I may have Christ.

Philippians 3:8

*H*ave you ever wished you had someone else's job? body shape? home? money?

I have. Why, just the other day, I remember thinking, *Wow, it'd be nice to be able to choose which days I want to work,* as Andee does.

Comparing ourselves with others isn't all bad—it can encourage us to make needed changes. But when we focus on what others have (and what we don't) and become envious, Scripture reminds us in Philippians 3:8 that these earthly things are really "garbage."

If you find yourself stuck in the comparison trap, here's help.

# The Comparison Trap

A friend called recently to tell me about a mutual acquaintance who has a new home, an expensive car and, it seems, the perfect family. My friend who phoned lives in a small house, drives an old car, and has a child who is in trouble. In her voice I could hear her sadness and disappointment with life.

After listening for a while, I told her about another conversation I'd just had with a woman whose husband had been killed in the prime of life, leaving her alone with two small children.

"You know," I gently reminded my friend on the phone, "it really makes a difference who we compare ourselves to."

That sentence jolted my friend out of her self-pity and depression. It helped her realize her life wasn't that bad after all!

I, too, have compared myself with others. For years I struggled over my inability to have a child. Whenever I'd see other women with young children, I'd long for a baby and tell myself, *I'll get pregnant next month.* I waited and waited for God to come through, but when nothing—not even adoption—seemed to work out for us, eventually I became angry with God over what I didn't have. I was afraid to admit it to anyone, including myself.

Then one day it struck me that life was passing me by—and I wasn't living. I finally realized I had to tell God how I felt. I sobbed and sobbed, telling him I loved him, and that I was sorry for being angry with him.

Around this time, I also read a good antidote (I'm just sorry I can't remember the author) to the comparison trap of envy—compassion. "Envy stares at someone else and thinks, *I wish I had what you have.* Compassion gazes at a person and asks, *What do I have that I can give to you?* Envy dwells on *poor me.* Compassion focuses on *poor them.* Envy destroys me, paralyzes me. Compassion rebuilds me, energizes me. Envy is a deadly sin; compassion is a wonderful Christlike virtue." I knew what I needed to do was focus not on what I didn't have but on what I did have.

> *Shared joy is more worthwhile—and ultimately more fun—than competitive envy.*
> DANDI DALEY MACKALL

Do you envy someone who's taller, slimmer, or younger? Do you wish you had a better-paying job, a husband, or a more wonderful husband? Or do you compare yourself with someone who lives in a beautiful house, has perfect children, and has a doctorate degree?

I've found that thanking God for his gifts helps me focus on the blessings in my life I can so easily take for granted—things like food to eat, a bed to sleep in, and family and friends who love me.

What are you thankful for today? As you consciously fill your mind with the good things God's given you, there'll be no more room for envy. And even if your family or job situation isn't all you wish it to be, there's still one thing to be grateful for: Life. After all, it's one of the greatest gifts God gives. *Elizabeth Mittelstaedt*

# A STEP FURTHER

## Envy Antidotes

1. *Evaluate who or what you're envious of—and why.* Putting a finger on the reason for your jealousy can help you put that emotion in perspective.
2. *Make needed changes in your life, if that's what God is calling you to do.* If you envy a friend who always seems to be organized, even with two small children, ask yourself, *What steps can I take in my life to be more organized?* If you envy a friend who's losing weight, then begin your own weight-loss program.
3. *Set about the business of helping others.* If you're not focused on yourself, it's amazing how quickly envy can disappear.
4. *Choose one thing to praise God for every day.* If you do this for a month, you'll set a pattern of praise rather than envy.

RCT

## Faith Focus

Are you, or have you ever been, stuck in a comparison trap? If so, who or what do you find yourself envying? Which of the four "Envy Antidotes" could you tackle this week to get yourself out of the trap and onto a healthier path?

### Prayer Pointer

Spend your time praising God for all the wonderful things he's done for you and the earthly possessions he's put in your care. Most of all, thank him for the gift of his Son—the gift that frees us to live with eternity in mind.

SHE IS CLOTHED WITH STRENGTH

AND DIGNITY, AND SHE LAUGHS

WITH NO FEAR OF THE FUTURE.

PROVERBS 31:25

*H*ave you ever been around a person who just tickles your funny bone? Maybe she shares hilarious stories over lunch or at the church picnic. Or she cracks a joke that makes you laugh even a bad day away.

Such people grasp the wisdom of verses on laughter, such as Proverbs 31:25. In fact, they know that the happiest people are those who not only laugh but *choose* to laugh—even in dire circumstances. Laughter sweeps away the gloom and paints our world in brighter colors.

Laughter *is* the best kind of medicine.

# Go Ahead! Laugh It Up!

Has there ever been a time in your life when you faced so much stress and pressure you didn't know what to do with it?

The year I graduated from college, I began working forty hours a week at a local mission, helping them organize their Volunteer Ministries, and also took three graduate-school night classes at two different universities. Three days a week, I was gone from home from 7:30 A.M. until almost midnight. The other days I worked at the mission, then studied all night and every weekend. My roommate, Corinne, and I also coordinated our church's singles ministry and cotaught junior-high Sunday school.

It was a recipe for exhaustion. But during that time we also had a dear Christian friend who spent time with my roommate and me. When school got overwhelming, he literally dragged me away from my studies to build a snowman in front of my apartment building. He was full of fun ideas, hilarious stories, and laughter. His upbeat presence helped keep me sane in those long months of grad school.

So what did I do? Three years later I married him! Now I never lack for laughter—and our home brims with it.

My husband, Jeff, has taught me more than anyone else the importance of laughter. It dispels gloom, brightens a difficult day, and can make even news such as, "Your car needs a thousand dollars of work," palatable.

It's so easy for me to take life too seriously, so I've made a point of surrounding myself with friends like Corinne and Jeff who have a sense of humor. They provide balance to my life, encourage me to evaluate when I take on too many projects at once (something I tend to do), and help me see that often the difficulty that's under my nose can be overcome if I just step back, evaluate it, then let the stress roll off with a good belly laugh. Funny how the easy presence of laughter can relax you enough to help you think of ways to solve a problem that otherwise might have taken hours of being hunched over a desk!

> *If we ask a creative God, he will help us open his gift box of laughter. He'll give us the ability to use laughter to bring sunshine to the dark days and added joy to the good ones.*
> CAROLE MAYHALL

Even in the worst of times, you can generate laughter. For instance, when Jeff's father was dying of cancer, we spent long hours with him in his home and hospital room, reading the Psalms for comfort. But we also interviewed him about his life, the funny things that had happened to him, his favorite expressions, and other memories. Those interviews became a scrapbook of delight—our gift to him his last Christmas—and then gave others comfort and chuckles during his memorial service. Even now, several years later, we laugh as a family over some of those memories.

What difficulties do you face today? Don't forget the healing nature of laughter—even if it seems you have to generate it for a while. The more you practice, the easier it will become. And as you pass it on to others, you'll discover that laughter not only benefits you but also livens up your relationships.

So go ahead—laugh it up! It's good for you.

*Ramona Cramer Tucker*

# A Step Further

## A Laugh a Day

1. *Post cartoons and funny stories on your refrigerator.*
2. *Buy an annual tear-off humor calendar.* Read one page a day in the morning or over lunch.
3. *Slip a surprise funny into your child's, husband's, or roommate's lunch bag.*
4. *Have a "laugh session" once a week.* Select a night and have family members or friends tell the funniest story they know.
5. *Watch and interact with children.* They're natural entertainers, and they show delight over the simplest things.
6. *Do what makes you laugh.* Have a tickle fest, start a pillow fight, or watch a really cheesy movie—just for the fun of it!
                                                    RCT

## Faith Focus

How often do you laugh—and at what? What steps can you take today to bring the gift of healthy, healing laughter into your everyday life?

*Prayer Pointer*

Thank God for being the Creator of humor! Ask him to help you be more aware of the funny things he brings into your day just to lighten it up. Praise him for the balance that healthy, healing laughter brings into your life.

THE APOSTLES RETURNED TO JE-
SUS FROM THEIR MINISTRY TOUR
AND TOLD HIM ALL THEY HAD
DONE AND WHAT THEY HAD
TAUGHT. THEN JESUS SAID,
"LET'S GET AWAY FROM THE
CROWDS FOR A WHILE AND REST."
THERE WERE SO MANY PEOPLE
COMING AND GOING THAT JESUS
AND HIS APOSTLES DIDN'T EVEN
HAVE TIME TO EAT. THEY LEFT BY
BOAT FOR A QUIETER SPOT.

MARK 6:30-32

*D*eadlines. Laundry. Church activities. Family and friend time. With such daily "to dos," it's no wonder we sometimes want to yell, "Stop the world! I want to get off!" Even Jesus and his apostles weren't immune—they needed to get away too.

At those times, I think of six-year-old Stephanie. When she needs to rest, her mother sends her to her room for a "time-out": a nap or a time of quiet play.

If you need a break, consider giving yourself a time-out—they're for adults, too! Here's what one person discovered when she was forced to take a break.

# Taking Time Out

"For the next six weeks, you'll have nothing to do but get well."

My doctor made that statement as though I'd just won a thousand dollars—but I wasn't so enthusiastic.

"I don't have *time* to do nothing!" I protested, thinking about the deadlines I had to meet, the son I had to outfit for college, the wedding gifts I needed to purchase, the errands I had to run. Productivity was in my bones, but this time I didn't have a choice—surgery was imminent, and I had to be ready by 8:00 A.M. the next Monday.

For years, I'd stuffed a file folder with quotes about rest. Notes tacked to my office bulletin board or on the refrigerator reminded me of its importance in God's design. But reading words on an index card is quite different from acting upon them. During my first days home from the hospital, I had to tell myself: *There is nothing I need to do today.* It was not an easy step.

But during those six weeks, I began praising God for the basics of life I had often been too distracted to notice. A bird's song. Pink roses in the garden. Dinner from a friend. A cup of hot tea from my husband. Simple, basic, thoughtful touches. Now I noticed them—and thanked God for them.

I also had time to tune in to my heavenly Father. As I recuperated, I thought about him often. I saw him in new ways through the pages of Scripture. I talked to him while I walked slowly down the street and around the block.

Eventually, my recuperation ended. I turned the pages of my calendar with some trepidation. Would I be able to sustain what I'd learned about taking time out in the midst of fast-paced living—which I knew was sure to return?

Six months have passed since then. I've returned to life as it was—but some things are different. My forced rest taught me how much I need that kind of time each day. Now, the hour just before I go to bed has become my daily "time-out." I tell myself: *There is nothing more I should be doing.* I enjoy some of my favorite things: soaking in a bubble bath, browsing through my magazines, sipping tea, reading my Bible. And in case you think my life is idyllic, often these time-outs happen in the middle of motion and commotion. Football games on TV. Stereos from upstairs bedrooms. Phones. Doorbells. Someone yelling, "Mom, where's my white shirt?"

*The more we allow ourselves to shut off the noise of the world, the less important the things of this life become and the more we want to please God, to live according to his standards.*

KAY ARTHUR

I'm learning that it *is* possible to find time out in the middle of normal, busy schedules. How? By realizing that taking time out is as much about what happens *inside* me as about the conditions around me. If I wait until the conditions are right, time-outs will never happen. But with determination and a little creativity, everyone can have the time. Don't wait for a forced time-out to discover how important God's plan for rest really is!

*Ruth Senter*

# A STEP FURTHER

## Pamper Yourself!

1. *Read a good book.* Curl up in a chair with a soothing beverage and enjoy this blessed time of quietness.
2. *Try a new hobby or take a class you've longed to take.* It'll relax you and also stimulate your personal growth.
3. *Arrange lunch with a friend.* Go out so you don't have to clean up dishes.
4. *Get a massage.* Style your hair differently, or get your first manicure. Put scent in your bathwater—anything that makes you feel special.
5. *Write uplifting Bible promises on index cards.* Carry one around with you for a week and read it once a day. One of my favorites is, "I can do everything with the help of Christ who gives me the strength I need" (Phil. 4:13).     RCT

## Faith Focus

When was the last time you took a "time-out"—just for you? What steps can you take today (even on a small scale) to ensure that you're able to give yourself some pampering on a regular basis?

### Prayer Pointer

Ask God today to renew your strength, to encourage you in your daily tasks, to help you prioritize your schedule, and to give you the restful moments you need to rejuvenate yourself and grow closer to him.

AND THE PROPHET ISAIAH SAID,
"THE HEIR TO DAVID'S THRONE
WILL COME, AND HE WILL RULE
OVER THE GENTILES. THEY WILL
PLACE THEIR HOPES ON HIM." SO I
PRAY THAT GOD, WHO GIVES YOU
HOPE, WILL KEEP YOU HAPPY AND
FULL OF PEACE AS YOU BELIEVE IN
HIM. MAY YOU OVERFLOW WITH
HOPE THROUGH THE POWER OF
THE HOLY SPIRIT.

ROMANS 15:12-13

- *I just know it'll be bad.*
- *Nothing good will ever come of this.*
- *I might as well give up now.*
- *We'll never get out of this financial hole.*

Negative thinking taints our lives, painting a picture of despair and hopelessness. Yet God calls us, as Christians, to "overflow with hope," even in tough times. However, he doesn't ask us to do it alone. He gives us "the power of the Holy Spirit."

If you think the worst first, here's how to move toward a hope-filled life.

# Are You a Negaholic?

Two Christmases ago, sick in bed with the flu, I passed the time by watching a talk show on "negaholism." One guest in particular stands out in my mind.

"I'm no good. I can't do anything right," she repeated. "I have no goals, and I know I can't change. My family would be better off without me."

I grew frustrated by this woman's self-loathing. *She's obviously not a Christian*, I thought smugly.

But the program stayed with me. It made me think about the times I've reacted with near-fatalism to certain situations in my life. Only a year ago, a routine mammogram sent me into an emotional tailspin as I agonized over the "what ifs" and anticipated the worst. My child's listlessness can conjure up fears about serious diseases. And what about those electromagnetic power lines right next to my office—could I be zapped with lightning as I walk to my car on a rainy day?

It's hard to admit, but despite a decades-old faith in Christ, at times I really don't differ from the self-proclaimed "negaholic" on that talk show.

Beyond the burden of defeat or depression, negaholism can cripple us with fear and leave us feeling separated from God and often missing out on the joy our Christian walk should bring. Habitual negativism is at odds with faith in Christ—a faith that teaches us that "with God everything is possible" (Matt. 19:26) and to "give your burdens to the Lord" (Ps. 55:22).

But before we can deal with negativism, we need to ferret out the underlying attitude or problem it may be hiding. "Whenever I counsel a negative person," says Dr. Ray

Mitsch, a clinical psychologist with the New Life Clinic in Wheaton, Illinois, "I like to ask her, 'What do you gain from this behavior?' A person who finds something wrong with everything frequently is looking for attention from the people around her."

Often our negative habits are old-fashioned sin: a self-centered heart, a lack of faith in God's sovereignty in our lives and the lives of those around us. In the end, pessimism is disagreeing with God, in effect telling God he doesn't know what's going on. And the only surefire remedy for these maladies is a healthy dose of confession and repentance.

*When I was little, it was hard to communicate because I was deaf. Sometimes I felt lonely. Today I hope when people hear me speak, they will never doubt they can do anything.*

HEATHER WHITESTONE

While God doesn't call us to blind optimism, he does call us to what Sheri Klinka, program director for the New Life Clinic's day hospital and a licensed social worker, calls "whatever" faith—trusting God no matter what. He wants us to be willing to see our health, our jobs, our relationships, our futures, even the world around us, with a perspective that mirrors his own.

That kind of change may seem overwhelming. But the gospel is filled with the promise of transformation. It may not happen overnight, but when we bolster our decision to change with prayer and the power of his Word, our dependence on God's perspective—instead of a "negaholic" one—will steadily grow.          *Jane Johnson Struck*

# A Step Further

### Be a Positive Thinker!

1. *Distance yourself emotionally.* When you're in the midst of worry, it's difficult to assess whether or not you have a legitimate reason for concern. Seek the counsel and prayers of friends for a balanced view.
2. *Determine your motive.* Is your pessimism triggered by disappointment over relationships or anger with God? Locating the cause makes it easier to develop a solution.
3. *Pinpoint the distortions.* List your fears, and compare them to the truth of God's Word .
4. *Face your fears.* Think about your biggest fear—then remember that God has promised to be with you and equip you in every situation. Choose to trust this truth.                    JJS

## Faith Focus

On a scale of one ("negaholism") to ten ("whatever" faith), where would you rate yourself? What will you do the next time negaholism grabs hold of you? In what areas do you need to develop a "whatever" faith?

### Prayer Pointer

Thank God for the many hopeful promises in his Word—and especially for his promise to take you home to heaven someday! Ask him to help you look at any difficulties with eternity in mind. Pray that he'll assist you in developing a "whatever" faith.

Listen to me, all you who are left in Israel. I created you and have cared for you since before you were born. I will be your God throughout your lifetime—until your hair is white with age. I made you, and I will care for you. I will carry you along and save you.

Isaiah 46:3-4

$\mathcal{M}$arianne is extraordinarily gifted. She's a top-notch research scientist, a brilliant musician, and is extremely creative in caring for her home and nurturing her relationships. How she gets all this done is beyond comprehension.

Looking at Marianne's talents, it'd be easy to feel chagrined at what you *don't* get done. But the books of Isaiah and Jeremiah remind us of how much God cares for us, *specifically*—and that he had a unique purpose for creating each one of us.

If you wonder why God hasn't gifted you as much as someone else, here's help.

# If You Think You're Nothing Special, Think Again!

Knotted embroidery threads and tubes of puffy paint filled my closet, waiting for that "someday" when I would transform them into glorious works of art.

But it never happened. Cross-stitch projects mysteriously acquired shapes previously unimagined by human minds. Puffy paint landed in daubs instead of designs on sweatshirts. How could it be so easy for others and so impossible for me?

One day I asked God why he'd made me so ordinary. I picked up my Bible and read, "Don't cherish exaggerated ideas of yourself or your importance, but try to have a sane estimate of your capabilities" (Rom. 12:3, Phillips).

I realized it's a mistake to compare myself to others. God says he has a unique purpose for my life, and he created me with everything I need to fulfill it (Eph. 2:10). If I'm missing particular gifts—like artistic skills—I won't need them to accomplish what God has in mind for me.

But before I could discover God's plans for me, I had to relinquish my own. Years ago, I went to Africa as a missionary nurse with grand dreams of a medical ministry. But it never even began. My three preschoolers needed help adjusting to our transcontinental move. And all day, every day, an unending stream of national children came to my kitchen door asking for cold water to drink. I couldn't get anything else done!

*God, you didn't bring me all the way to Africa just to pass out water, did you?* I asked.

*If I did, and that's all I ever ask you to do, will you do it?* I sensed God reply.

But anybody could pass out water, I thought. I wanted a *real* job. Yet God's ways are not my ways, and his thoughts are not my thoughts (Isa. 55:8). Finally, in faith, I laid down my dreams and took up his opportunities—ordinary, everyday cups of water. And slowly I realized that serving these kids and the other African people who steadily streamed through our house utilized the gifts of welcoming unexpected guests, feeling sympathy, cooking, and talking that God had graciously bestowed upon me. Even though these jobs didn't seem special, I learned that God uses seemingly small things to build his kingdom. Two of those national children looking for a cup of water are now my adopted sons.

> *There is nothing so beautiful as a confident woman, one who can love because she knows she is loved.*
> INGRID TROBISCH

Today my closet bulges with new "someday" projects. Recipes I'll most definitely try "as soon as I have time." Bible studies I wrote years ago for my study group that are now being published. But these are challenges I enjoy rather than dread.

Learning what I'm gifted in has led me to heartfelt yeses—and the liberating sense of finding my specific niche in God's kingdom. Learning what I'm *not* gifted in has led to wonderfully guilt-free noes (most days)! I've discovered it's a lot more fun being who God made me instead of trying to be someone else! **Ruth Van Reken**

# A Step Further

## Making the Best of Your Gifts

1. *Make a list.* In one column list things that you enjoy doing and that come easily to you. In the other, scribble down things you don't like to do or that are difficult for you.
2. *Use your gifts.* Look at the list of things that come naturally to you, and brainstorm ways to utilize these gifts—no matter how big or small the task may seem.
3. *Ask God how you can serve him right now.* Pray for guidance, and then do whatever he reveals to you.
4. *Stop trying to be what you're not.* You'll only be frustrated if you try to do things God hasn't asked or equipped you to do.

RVR

## Faith Focus

Have you identified your "gifted" areas? If not, perhaps you'll want to try one of the "Identify and Use Your Gifts" tips this week. If you do know what you're good at, how do you see those gifts—as behind the scenes and unimportant or granted especially to you by a loving God? What's one way you could use your gifts to encourage someone today?

### Prayer Pointer

Thank God for knowing you so well that he gifted you perfectly. Ask him to reveal to you what you're good at, then to help you discover ways in which you can use those gifts to make an eternal difference.

# ACKNOWLEDGMENTS

*Today's Christian Woman* magazine and Tyndale House Publishers would like to thank TCW staff members Barbara Calvert, Camerin J. Courtney, and Joy McAuley for their help in the editorial/permission process, and the following people who graciously gave their permission to adapt the following material from *Today's Christian Woman* in this book.

Budzowski, Bonnie. "Loneliness . . . Can It Be a Gift?" (September/October 1995).

Carter, Betty Smartt. "Confessions of a TV Addict" (September/October 1993).

Clark, Mary Roberts. "The Day I Kept My Mouth Shut" (November/December 1995).

Crockett, Marsha. "Home Beautiful" (September/October 1997).

Grissom, Suzanne M. "Confessions of a Woman on the Whirl" (July/August 1995).

Halseide, Michele. "If Only I Had . . ." (March/April 1992); "People-Pleaser or God-Pleaser?" (July/August 1992).

Harris, Janis Long. "Who Am I *Really?*" (March/April 1992).

Higgs, Liz Curtis. "Say WHAT?" (January/February 1997).

Jaeger, Paige. "I Want! I Want! I Want!" (November/December 1989).

Johnson, Jan. "Shy like Me" (May/June 1991).

Mackall, Dandi Daley. "Good Gossip" (March/April 1995).

Mathers, Mayo. *AfterWords*, "Taming the Tongue" (March/April 1996).

Mayhall, Carole. "How Honest Is Too Honest?" (November/December 1989).

Mittelstaedt, Elizabeth. "The Comparison Trap" (March/April 1995).

Newenhuyse, Elizabeth Cody. "The Truth about Exaggeration" (January/February 1993); "Cultivating Contentment" (September/October 1995); "Promises, Promises . . ." (July/August 1997).

Patterson, Lauretta. "No Time to Entertain?" (January/February 1991).

Senn, Jan L. Interview with Carol Kent, "Carol Kent on Keeping Confident!" (January/February 1995).

Senter, Ruth. "The Splendor of the Ordinary" (May/June 1989); "Time Out" (May/June 1993).

Struck, Jane Johnson. "Are YOU a Negaholic?" (November/December 1991); Interview with Francine Rivers, *One Woman's Story*, "Hooked on Romance" (May/June 1995).

Tada, Joni Eareckson. "We Will Be Whole" (March/April 1991).

Van Reken, Ruth. "If You Think You're 'Nothing Special,' Think Again . . ." (January/February 1996).

Wright, Vinita Hampton. "Forgiveness: Sounds Great . . . but Does It Really Work?" (November/December 1995).